# SAMUEL NUTT
# (c.1675-1738)

*and the*

# FRENCH CREEK
# IRON-WORKS

*at Coventry, Chester County, Pennsylvania*

## A BIOGRAPHICAL AND HISTORICAL SKETCH

## SAMUEL NUTT AND THE FRENCH CREEK IRON-WORKS AT COVENTRY, CHESTER COUNTY, PENNSYLVANIA

by Daniel A. Graham

Copyright: 2017 Friends of Hopewell Furnace National Historic Site
Cover Photo: by Peggy Hartzel, Coventry Monument in Warwick Park

Library of Congress Number: 2017918250
International Standard Book Number: 978-1-60126-559-3

Please cross reference under:
Coventry Forge
Robert Grace (1709-1766)
Rebecca (Savage) Nutt Grace
Mordecai Lincoln
Reading Furnace
Rock Run Furnace
Samuel Savage
Warwick Furnace

**Masthof Press**
219 Mill Road | Morgantown, PA 19543-9516
www.Masthof.com

# THE FRIENDS OF HOPEWELL FURNACE

Add your support to the non-profit group that speaks out on your behalf to promote, protect and preserve the natural, historical, cultural and recreational resources of Hopewell Furnace National Historic Site. Becoming a member demonstrates your commitment to the shared stewardship of this national park.

A successful Hopewell Furnace doesn't just happen; it reflects the loyalty and support of its dedicated members. These are people who not only appreciate the Furnace's importance and inspiration, but also the quality of life and sense of community it provides. Join today to enjoy the opportunities and benefits exclusive to the Friends of Hopewell Furnace.

Visit our website, www.friendsofhopewellfurn.org, to stay up to date on current activities, to browse the Hopewell Ledgers database and to explore programs of interest.

# TABLE OF CONTENTS

# FOREWORD

*"Samuel Nutt, Jr, left no son,*
*and the name became extinct in that family."*
HISTORY OF CHESTER COUNTY

This publication was written while I was doing research on the events that led to the building of Warwick Furnace in Chester County. Although Samuel Nutt died before Warwick was constructed, it was his vision, presented in his will, which requested that it be built. His French Creek Iron-Works were Reading and Warwick Furnace's predecessor. To understand those furnaces, you have to understand both the history of the complex at French Creek and the relationship between Nutt and William Branson. Consequently, this work on the French Creek Iron-Works and Nutt's involvement in them provides a backdrop for and essential information on Warwick. But, more importantly, it also serves as a stand-alone book to document Samuel Nutt's life, the beginnings of the Chester County iron industry and the various ironworks at the French Creek forks. I have written works on Thomas Rutter, Samuel Savage, and Thomas Potts. This book on Samuel Nutt completes the biographies of the early Pennsylvania ironmasters.

Most of the early information that has been presented on Samuel Nutt's life and the French Creek ironworks in secondary sources comes almost completely from two publications: the early and well-distributed 1874 *The Memorial of Thomas Potts Junior* by Isabella (Batchelder) James; and the 1881 *The History of Chester County, Pennsylvania* by J. Smith Furthey and Gilbert Cope. Both have a good amount of primary information and are routinely copied by later works. Neither provide references although Furthey and Cope obtained a good bit of their information about Nutt from the Taylor papers at the Historical Society of

Pennsylvania. Both books have been used almost as primary resources. The uneven 1914 *Forges and Furnaces in the Province of Pennsylvania* does a good job in combining information from both sources into one write-up but provides nothing new.

Two publications that are more recent provide biographies and have additional information on Nutt: the 1997 *Lawmakers and Legislators in Pennsylvania, 1710-1756*, has a biography on him and Estelle Cremer's 2003 *Coventry the Skool Kill District* presents information on him, Coventry Township and the ironworks there. Additionally, a delightful 2007 book by a local author, *Message by Horseback*, provides a good overview of the Nutt forge material and a 1976 book (reprinted and revised in 2016) by the East Nantmeal Historic Commission, *The Forgers*, provides information on the Coventry area.

Nutt was a Quaker at immigration and appears to have remained a nominal Friend for some time. Quaker minister, Thomas Chakley, visited his works in 1726, and had "a large, quite, solid meeting" there. However, other than his certificate of removal from Coventry Meeting in England, which was recorded at Concord Meeting in Chester County, records are silent as to Nutt's attendance at any meetings. While no documentation has been uncovered, Nutt is said to have eventually joined the 7th Day Baptist English congregation on French Creek. He served in numerous responsible public positions and was an acknowledged leader in early Chester County during his life.

While his life is documented, Nutt's ironworks are less so. Perhaps this paper's main contribution is to sort out some of the confusion. It is a fair statement that we don't know the exact beginning or ending dates of any of his works. What is usually provided is the information found in the above-mentioned Chester County history. Nutt was involved in building two forges, two cold-blast furnaces and a steel furnace on the French Creek along what is now Rt. 23 west of Rt. 100 at Coventryville. No physical structures remain of any of them and with the exception of Coventry Forge, which stayed active until the mid-1800s, their locations are educated guesses. The ironworks get confused and often intermingled in various write-ups. Similarly, although his estate inventory indicates he made stove plates and stoves, there are no known ones in existence with Nutt's name on them. There was a stove plate discovered with the name "Christeen" on it, which was thought by Henry Mercer to be an early name for the first blast furnace at Coventry. However, it is perhaps a name for Nutt and Branson's Christiana Creek furnace that they owned in conjunction with several other ironmasters and from which Coventry Forge received pig iron.

Several ledger books for Nutt-era works are known to exist, the earliest being Coventry Account Book B, dated 1727-1732, that is located at the Historical Society of Pennsylvania. Without doubt, Samuel Nutt was the second person in Pennsylvania to produce iron. Although 1718 is generally the date given for when the Coventry bloomery first produced iron, "there seems to be some uncertainty and obscurity about the time." Nutt and Branson's partnership dates and who owned what percentage and when, are at this time guesses. However, in 1744, probably as a part of sueing Nutt's heirs, William Branson filed a number of legal documents that are found in the Letters of Attorney books in Harrisburg. They provide otherwise unattainable information on the relationship of Nutt and Branson (and Moredecai Lincoln), the ironwork dates and ownership percentages and have been used in this paper.

The earliest contempory source uncovered mentioning Nutt's first forge is 1720. Assuming he followed Thomas Rutter's example across the Schuylkill, the first ironwork Nutt built was probably a bloomery forge, although Cremers suggests that it may have been a Catalan forge. However, like Rutter (his future father-in-law), Nutt quickly moved to the more efficient two-step iron making process. In 1720, Nutt formed a partnership to obtain capital and technical help and built a second forge. By 1725, he had formed another partnership and was the moving force in building a cold-blast furnace on Rock Run and converting his bloomery forge to a refinery forge. What role his later partner, William Branson, played in the construction other than capitalizing these works is unknown. This combination of a furnace and forge, along with the buildings, sheds, and houses was named by Nutt the French Creek Iron-Works and was called that during its existance. This name has been largely forgotton and the works were simply called "Coventry" by later sources. The complex produced iron until the two partners split—each to their own furnace—Branson moving to Reading, and Nutt's heirs building Warwick Furnace. The refinery forge, Coventry, became part of the Warwick complex and remained active on-and-off, until the mid-1800s.

Probably one of the best overview presentations to attempt to unravel the ironworks' evolution and locations is a chapter in an unlikely 1936 book by Chester County lawyer, district attorney and local historian, Wilmer MacEltree, entitled *Around the Boundaries of Chester County.* MacEltree tried to untangle Coventry's early history and plotted the location of the various works. He provides a thoughtful presentation on their locations but his lack of references is frustrating.

Trying to sort out Samuel Nutt's various land transactions is challenging. In his lifetime, he obtained almost 3,000 acres—mostly in Coventry and Nantmeal by warrant and patent. In this paper, I tried to concentrate on presenting the histories of his initial land acquisitions—his ore mine, ironwork and what became the Warwick tract. Nutt filed for two warrants in 1717 and 1718 and that produced three separate tracts of land. There is some confusion if his 300-acre ironwork tract at the forks of the French Creek came from a 400-acre warrant or an 800-acre one and I have tried to sort it out.

More than the normal interest has been generated in Nutt's Coventry ironworks because about 1720 he went into partnership with Mordecai Lincoln, the sixteenth president's great-great-grandfather. Lincoln lived at the forge from 1720 to 1725. Although the partnership was short-lived, the inclusion of Lincoln has added a spotlight to the ironwork and generated some research that otherwise would not have been done. There has been a lack of research on Nutt because he had no descendants. Iron industry researchers have provided what information there is on him. The recent popularity in genealogy has been a prime source in collecting information about one's ancestors, no matter how small of a detail. Nutt has missed this scrutiny.

There has been some historical confusion if Samuel Nutt had any interest in Reading Furnace, which was built about 1736, upstream from Coventry on French Creek. The story that has generally been presented is Nutt's partner, William Branson, broke off on his own and built the well-known Reading Furnace. Reading Furnace biographer, Estelle Cremers, in her book, *Reading Furnace 1736*, supports this version. But several earlier secondary sources state Nutt was involved with this furnace. It comes down to whether the original furnace on Rock Run near Coventry was replaced by a second furnace, which was called Reading, or whether Samuel Nutt had an interest in Reading Furnace that Branson is associated with. I also sort that out in this paper.

Although partially covered in Part II, brief histories of Reading Furnace, Warwick Furnace and Coventry Forge are provided in the Appendix along with the wills of Samuel Nutt, Anna Nutt and Samuel Savage.

I would like to dedicate this paper to the late Estelle Cremers, who as in all things northern Chester County, paved the way before us. I would like to thank the folks at the Chester County Historical Society for their help in researching Nutt and also Jonathan Strayer and Aaron McWilliams at the Pennsylvania Archives who were extremely helpful in navigating the collections there and for locating the lost Nutt material in the Letters of Attorney. Ann Bedrick, Kristine Gordon-Watson, Allison Mallimo and Maureen Noonan from the East Nantmeal Historical Commission were a joy to deal with. Thanks to Jay Erb at Warwick Park and Peggy Hartzel for supplying pictures and to Tom Walsh who teaches Chester County history for various suggestions. Additionally, thanks to Gene Delaplane, Elizabeth Santos, Elliott Segal and Nancy Dooling for their review of the paper. Finally, thanks to the Friends of Hopewell Furnace for publishing it and special thanks to Peter Hammond for editing the entire document.

*-Dan Graham, 2017*

# PENSYLVANIA, NOVA JERSEY ET NOVA YORK CUM REGIONIBUS AD FLUVIUM DELAWARE IN AMERICA SITIS

German Map showing Reding (Reading) Furnace and Warwick Furnace, c.1748 by Tobias Conrad Lotter 1717-1777, Created/Published Aug. Vind. [Augsburg, Germany: s.n., 1748?]

# INTRODUCTION

*"That Whereas ye Petitioners haveing Laid out great sums of money To building and Errecting of Iron works for the making of Iron In this Country which said manufacturing must unavoidably advance the intrest of the same..."*

1726 ROAD PETITION FROM SAMUEL NUTT,
WILLIAM BRANSON AND JONATHAN ROBESON

Ironmaster Samuel Nutt lay dying at his home in Coventry, Chester County, when he wrote his will on September 25, 1737. Nutt, an English immigrant, had built Pennsylvania's second ironwork and Chester County's first near the forks of the French Creek at Coventry, about

1718. At his death, he was running one of the most successful iron and production systems in Pennsylvania. He had no children, but had five stepchildren by his wife, Anna (Rutter) Savage, the widow of Samuel Savage. One of Anna's daughters, Rebecca, married his nephew and heir, Samuel Nutt, Jr., whom Nutt had brought over from England to help run the works. By 1723, Nutt had built two forges on French Creek and a furnace on Rock Run. His original ironwork was a bloomery forge but he had quickly taken on partners and the company built a cold-blast charcoal furnace and a refinery forge creating what was called the French Creek Iron-Works. Because the furnace was closed by 1750 and the finery forge, called Coventry, continued well into the 19th century, the generic term given in later publications to describe the complex was "the Coventry Works."

By the time of his death in 1738, Nutt had had a falling out with his partner, William Branson, apparently over the boundaries of their various land acquisitions that were very much intertwined. In 1736, Branson and Nutt built a new cold-blast furnace under their partnership called "Redding" to replace the original one on Rock Run. Branson, however, outside of the partnership, without Nutt, built another Reading Furnace on French Creek upstream from the Coventry Works on his land. These two separate furnaces, both near each other, were apparently given the same name that would cause confusion as to their histories. Nutt decided he would also build a separate furnace without Branson but his illness intervened before it could be built. His will left his wife 120 acres of land on the north side of the South Branch of French Creek between Reading and Coventry: "in Such a place as she shall think proper to Build a Furnace on." This furnace was indeed built and became one of the largest producers of pig iron in Pennsylvania and the colonies. They named it Warwick, in honor of Nutt's English home.

This is the story of Samuel Nutt, his role in founding the early iron industry of Chester County, Pennsylvania, and the ironwork complex he built at French Creek.

# PART I

**EARLY LIFE, IMMIGRATION
AND FIRST FORGE,
c.1675-1724**

*Eighteenth Century Six Plate Stove side plate cast at Colebrookdale Furnace by Thomas Rutter. Courtesy of The Jacob Brothers Collection.*

# EARLY LIFE,
# IMMIGRATION

*"Coventry township doubtless received its name
from Samuel Nutt, an early settler who came
from Coventry, in Warwickshire, England."*
WILLIAM EGLE

*Samuel Nutt produced a certificate from the Monthly Meeting of Coven . . . held
of the 2 mo. 1714. which recommendeth as a Friend in Unity & clear on . . . accou . . .
marriage & also of a good conversation & serviceable amongst them . . .*

O n his arrival to Pennsylvania in 1714, Samuel Nutt (c.1675-1738)
was an unmarried Friend from Coventry, England. Coventry was
originally in Warwickshire but is now located in the West Midlands, 95
miles northwest of London. At that time, Coventry was the fourth largest
city in England. Nothing has been confirmed about Samuel Nutt's ancestry.[1]  Based on a woodcut of the arms of Nutt made from the original
brought from England, Isabella (Batchelder) James in her *Potts Memorial,*
indicates: "Family tradition asserts that he was the younger son of a bar-
onet; and the coat of arms he brought with him from England, a copy of
which is inserted in this volume, bears a crescent, the mark of a second
son."[2]  However, Nutt had another copy of a coat of arms in a book he
brought with him that was slightly different than Batchelder's and shows
the arms of Sir Thomas Nutt of Lewis in the County of Sussex.

Nutt apparently arrived in Philadelphia at age 39 alone, without other family members. His 1737 will did leave bequests to friends
in England.[3]  Although not much is known for sure about his life in

England, Samuel Nutt's writings show that he was educated and a deed shows that he was a weaver. At immigration, Nutt was a Quaker in good standing. His certificate of removal from the Coventry Friends Meeting indicates that he had a "Good Conversion." It would appear he became a Quaker by conversion but his family did not. Coventry Friends Meeting in Warwickshire, England, had been established in 1668, and Samuel Nutt was noted as a member there by 2nd month, 1698. Meeting records of that date show that Samuel Nutt was one of seventeen members of the meeting who were charged to "assist traveling Friends in their journey as it comes in course." He is also listed in their records as one of two men appointed to talk with a member who was given to "excessive drinking and frequenting ale houses."[4]

Samuel Nutt's date of birth is unknown but estimating that he was age 23 at the time of the meeting annotation, he would have been born c.1675. That he was able to purchase the rights to a sizeable tract of land in America before immigration would indicate that he was a man of means by that time.

Like many English Friends during this period, Nutt was persecuted for his religious beliefs during the reign of William of Orange. Under entries for Warwickshire, his name appeared with others for the year 1707 in Besse's *A Brief Account of Many of the Prosecutions of the People call'd Quakers*: "Stephen Scotten, Moses Merry, William Townsend, Richard Mallet, John Trustance, Samuel Nutt, John Brabins, Charles Higgenson, John Wicks and Susan King the Younger, of Coventry, were prosecuted in the Ecclesiastical Court for a Church Rate (so-called) at the Suit of the Wardens and Excommunicated."[5]

*Warwickshire.*

1707. Stephen Scotten, Moses Merry, William Townsend, Richard Mallett, John Trustance, Samuel Nutt, John Brabins, Charles Higginson, John Wicks and Susan King the Younger, of *Coventry*, were prosecuted in the *Ecclesiastical Court* for a Church-Rate (so called) at the Suit of the Wardens, and Excommunicated.

Samuel Nutt, listed as a "Weaver," was still in Coventry, England, on May 4, 1714, when he purchased by indenture of Benjamin Weight, Clothier, also of Coventry and Mary his wife, the rights to 1,250 acres in Pennsylvania. The deed does not provide an exact location of the property; it simply states that the land was located "in the Province of Pennsylvania." When Nutt took possession, this land would be partially located in Sadsbury Township in Chester County near the Lancaster County line.[6] He paid £60 lawful money for the property.

The January 25, 1714/15 [1715], will of Edward Bennett of Thornbury, mentions Nutt's ownership of this land and places it in Sadsbury. Bennett left son John Bennett 200 acres of land in Sadsbury, adjoining lands of George Leonard, **Samuel Nutt** and Thomas George. Nutt mortgaged some of this property on December 2, 1720, to Israel Taylor when he was building a second forge at Coventry. (Mortgage Book D, page 175) The 1720 indenture also notes the property was in Sadsbury and lists Nutt as a Yeoman:

> *THIS INDENTURE made the Second Day of December in the Year of our Lord one* thousand seven hundred & twenty BETWEEN Samuel Nutt of the County of Chester in the province of pennsylvania Yoman of the one part Israel Taylor of Tynnicum in the County and province aforesaid Chyrurgeon [surgeon] of the other part WITNESSETH that the said Samuel Nutt for and in Consideration of the Sum of Thirty Pounds of Lawful money of America to him in hand pay'd by the said Israel Taylor...HATH granted... unto the said Israel Taylor ALL that piece or parcel of land situate lying and being in the Township of Sadbury in the said County BEGINNING at a post and thence South Three hundred and forty eight perches by the land of William Brinton thence West by South one hundred and ninety three perches by vacant lands then north Three hundred forty eight perches by the land called Sarah Weights then east by north by vacant lands one hundred ninety three perches then to the place of beginning containing four hundred acres.[7]

It is assumed that Nutt immigrated to Pennsylvania shortly after his May 4th purchase. He presented a certificate from the Coventry Monthly Meeting dated 2mo [April] 7, 1714, to the Concord Monthly Meeting in Chester County, where it was recorded on 10mo [December] 13, 1714. This was the only time Samuel Nutt is mentioned in Concord records. In fact, he appears not to be mentioned again in any meeting records. Nutt's *Lawmaking & Legislators of Pennsylvania* biography states that: "His name has not been located in the minutes or records of any Friends Meetings in Chester or Philadelphia counties." His certificate states that he was recommended as a "Friend in Unity & clear on accounts and marriage" and "Serviceable" among them.[8]

Nutt brought with him a small personal book bound in parchment and fashioned with a copper clasp. It is inscribed: "Sam[ll] Nutt His Book 1702" and is worth mentioning. In addition to a family crest, it contains interesting facts, a number of recipes and various remedies for sundry ailments.[9] Currently located in the Chester County Historical Society, he entitled it: *Savorall Rare Sacrets and Choyce Curiossityes.* It has been listed as one of the earliest cookbooks in America.

Very little has been uncovered about Nutt's whereabouts between when his certificate was recorded at Concord Meeting in December 1714, and when he filed a warrant for his ore tract in September 1717. The Furthey and Cope history indicates in 1718, that he was listed as being of "Birmingham." He is noted in a release dated October 11, 1716. On that date, Margaret Miles, of the Township of Radnor, Widow, and Rice Thomas and Samuel Nutt, "now or late of the County of Philadelphia, in the said Province, Merchants," sold to Timothy Davis a tract of 500 acres in the Great Valley, in Chester County. This was the same property they had purchased on August 30, 1716, from Benjamin Davis. The property was bounded by the lands of John Evans and Hugh Samuel. *(Chester County Deed Bk. Q, Vol. 16,* pp. 266-269) It is assumed that Nutt took possession of his Chester County property in Sadsbury Township at immigration.[10] He sold most of his Sadsbury land rather quickly and it was to the forks of French Creek at what would become Coventry Township that he would turn his attention.

*Samuel Nutt's 1702 book titled* "Savorall Rare Sacrets and Choyce Curiossityes" *is currently located at the Chester County Historical Society.* Picture courtesy of Dan Graham.

# NUTT BUILDS A BLOOMERY FORGE AT COVENTRY, 1717-1720

*"It all started [the Chester County Iron Industry] with Nutt's iron ore mine."*

ARTHUR BINING

*"Friend's [French] Creek, in Chester County, near the Schuylkill. The mine is rich and abundant, from ten to twelve feet deep, commencing on the surface. Its discoverer is Mr. Nutt."*

ISRAEL ACRELIUS, 1759, *HISTORY OF NEW SWEDEN* [11]

Samuel Nutt didn't remain involved with the Sadsbury propery long, if at all. He decided to turn his interest to iron making in Coventry in northern Chester County. His immigration to Pennsylvania coincidently coincided with the founding of the iron industry there and he would become an important player in its early development. It was in this industry that Nutt quickly involved himself and with which his name would become synonymous.

In 1715, Thomas Rutter (1660-1730), Germantown blacksmith, Baptist minister, and Pennsylvania assemblyman, traveled up the Schuylkill River on the Manatawny Road and "on his own strength" built Pennsylvania's first charcoal ironwork on the north side of the river on the Manatawny Creek.[12]   This ironwork was originally situated in Amity Township and called Rutter's Bloomery. It was located northwest of present-day Pottstown and by 1716, Rutter was making iron. Jonathan Dickinson tells Jno. Askew about the building of the Rutter Forge:

> "Philada ye 5th of febury 1716/17" (1717),  This last Summer one Tho Rutter a Smith who Lives not farr from Jerman Town hath removed farther up in the Country & of his own Strength hath Sett upon making Iron. Such it proves to be as is highly Sett by All the Smiths here say that the best of Sweeds Iron Doth not Exceed it & we have accot of others that are going on wh Iron works. Its supposed Here is Stone Sufficient to Employ vast number of people for ages to come. The first projectors may open ye Way And in all Liklyhood Hemp & Iron may be Improved & Transported hence in time if not discouraged however a few years will supply this place for its domestic service may be Easily Supposed."[13]

## NUTT'S IRON MINE AT NANTMEAL, 1717

Taking his cue from Rutter, in 1717 and 1718, Nutt began warranting tracts of land on which he would build his iron empire. He initially filed two warrants that produced three tracts of land: one that would become his iron mine, one that he would build his ironworks on, and one for coaling that also became his Warwick Furnace seat in 1737. These were located in an isolated area at the forks of the French Creek in northern Chester County on the opposite side of the Schuylkill from Rutter.[14]  Township lines had not yet been set and the properties would end up in different townships. The tract containing iron ore deposits and the Warwick Tract became part of Nantmeal Township and the ironwork became part of Coventry Township; all were in Chester County. Because applications for warrants at that time were made at the Land Office in Philadelphia orally, we do not know the exact date he filed. In 1717,

Nutt applied for his warrant on the land he would establish his ore tract. He requested 400 acres.

There is an anecdotal story with several variations that continually is repeated of why Nutt chose this property to warrant and how he found it. The following is typical: "The ore bank at Coventry was discovered and pointed out to Nutt by an Indian chief, to whose daughter, in recognition, gave an iron pot worth four shillings six pence."[15] This tract was listed in Nantmeal Township by the 1722 taxes.[16]

On September 18th, 1717, the Commissioners of Property: Richard Hill, Isaac Norris and James Logan, issued a warrant to Jacob Taylor, the Surveyor General:

> "At the Request of Samuel Nutt of the County of Chester That we would Grant him to take up amongst the New Surveys made in the said County the quantity of four hundred Acres of Land for which he agrees to pay to the Propriety[rs.] use fforty Pounds Money of Pensilvania for the whole and the Yearly quitrent of one Shilling Sterling for each hundred Acres. These are to Authorize and Require thee to Survey or cause to be Survey'd unto the said Samuel Nutt in the said County of Chester According to the method of Townships appointed the Said quantity of ffour hundred Acres of Land that hath not been already Survey'd nor appropriated nor is Seated by the Indians and make Returns thereof into the Secretarys Office which Survey in case the Said Samuel fulfill the above agreement within three Months aff[r] the date hereof Shall be Valid otherwise the Same is to be Void as if it had never been made nor this Warrant ever granted. Given under our hands...the 18th day of September Anno Dobi 1717."

The Minutes for the Meeting of the Commissioners of Property dated "8th 2 month, 1717" show that a warrant was signed to Samuel Nutt for 400 acres: "back in Chester County for 400, the whole, and usual quitrent, to be paid in 3 months after the date of the Warr't, dated

the 18th of 7ber [September], 1717." While the warrant was for 400
acres, only 250 were surveyed the following month:

> "Surveyed the 28th of the 8th Month [October] 1717
> Pursuant to the Commissioners Warrt dated the 18th of Sep-
> tember 1717 unto Samuel Nut a Certain or Parcel of Land on
> a Small Branch of the ffrench Creek in the County of Chester...
> Containing Two hundred and fifty acres with the usual allow-
> ance of Six acres per Cent. Returned into the Secretary Office
> May 16th 1718. Jacob Taylor."[17]

A patent was requested August 20, 1718. However, Nutt did not receive his patent on the tract signed by the Proprietary until July 5th, 1736.[18]
Even then, there were problems. While Nutt had paid the Penns for the
land, he apparently by the time of his death had not paid all the quit-rents
required by the deed on the mine tract or for a survey on another tract. Long
after Nutt's death, the arrears were paid in 1774, by John Potts, Jr., who
was acting in a legal capacity for his brother Samuel, and brother-in-law
Thomas Rutter who then owned the mine tract and Warwick Furnace:

> "Philada. 2d. April 1774 received of Samuel Nutt by
> the hands of John Potts Esq the sum of One hundred and
> six Pounds 7 s. Current Monies of Pennsylvania in full for
> the Balance due on a Settlmt. of his Account with the Pro-
> prietaries this day including the arrears of Quitrent due the
> Proprietaries to the first of last month on 1150 acres of land
> confirmed to him by two patents each dated 11th 4 Mo,
> 1736 and also on a tract of 250 acres confirmed to him by
> Patent dated the 20th 6 Mo. 1718 lying in Nantmeal Town-
> ship Chester County. Recs. For the Hon. the Proprietaries.
> Edmun Physick."[19]

Nutt's original "mine hole" was on a small portion of the 250-acre
tract. On February 28, 1723/24, separate Articles of Agreement were
drawn up between Samuel Nutt and Mordecai Lincoln, and between

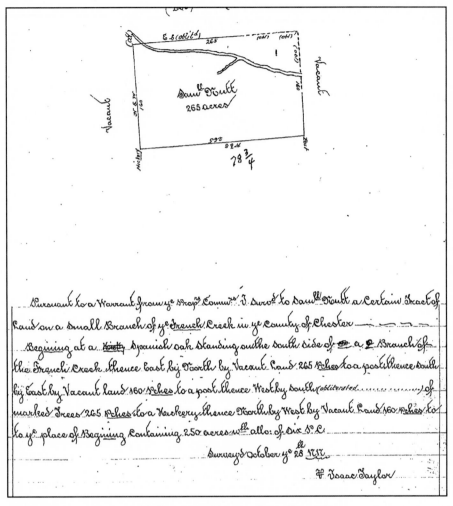

*Taylor 1717 Survey of Ore Tract* [20]

Nutt and William Branson selling each one-third of six acres of land "which Six Acres as now Laid out to be the same more or Less is Deemed to be one half of the Iron Mine." Both Lincoln and Branson paid Nutt £33, 6 shillings and 8 pence.[21] Of interest, because Nutt did not have a signed patent for the tract at that time, he could not legally transfer it.

The ore Nutt would use was extracted by trench mining, basically digging numerous holes or pits. Two men could provide enough ore for a typical cold blast furnace of that time. Swedish naturalist Peter Kalm visited Pennsylvania in 1748, and he gives a description of mining there during that period:

> "Iron is dug in such great quantities in Pennsylvania... The ore is here commonly infinitely easier got in the mines than our Swedish ore. For in many places, with a pick-ax, crow-foot, and a wooden club, it is got with the same ease with which a hole can be made in a hard soil: in many places the people know nothing of boring, blasting, and firing..."[22]

This ore deposit, which Nutt initially did not make part of the company, gave him a superior position in the partnership. His personal estate accounting in 1738 lists: "The mine tract consisting of 250 acres of land." It was located to the northwest of the confluence of the French Creek Branches near the Falls of French Creek about a mile north of Knauertown. The mine tract eventually became part of Warwick Township where it was located on the eastern edge of Warwick Village. Initially called the French Creek Iron Mine, the name eventually was changed to the Warwick Mines.

The iron deposit proved to be a very substantial bed and was mined for many years and eventually used by both Reading and Warwick Furnaces. The mine guaranteed the success of Nutt's iron endeavors at Coventry. The Swedish historian, Rev. Israel Acrelius, in his 1759 *History of New Sweden*, mentions the mine: "Friend's [French] Creek, in Chester County, near the Schuylkill. The mine is rich and abundant, from ten to twelve feet deep, commencing on the surface. Its discoverer is Mr. Nutt."[23]

The mine was also described by two other travelers at the end of the American Revolution. Swede Samuel Hermelin, who visited the mine in 1783, after the French Creek Works had closed and long after Nutt was dead, provides several pages in his book on the ore and mine. The mine at that time was known as the Warwick Ore Quarries as it was sending iron ore to Warwick Furnace. He notes: "Considerable quantities of iron have been dug out from this ore field during a period of from 40 to 50 years..." He also provides a good description of how the ore was mined:

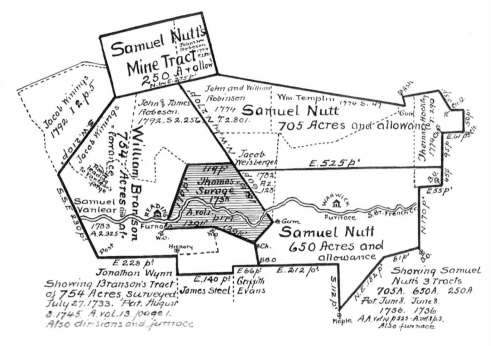

*Draught of mine tract also showing Reading and Warwick Furnaces.*[24]

The mine owner supplies the implements to the workmen, free of charge, which, however, consist of nothing but picks, sledges, and sieves [strainers], because blasting is not necessary. Also, water is kept away by the mine owner, who at each of these ore fields pays the monthly wage of a laborer at the handpumps....All ore [transported] from the Warwik mines to the blast furnace, which is two miles [distant], is conveyed by the manufacturers' own teams and people."[25]

Hessian doctor Johann David Schoepf agreed with Hermelin. Also visiting in 1783, he called them the "Warwick mine holes." He states: "Any knowledge of mining is superfluous here, where there is neither shaft nor gallery to be driven, all work being at the surface or in great, wide trenches or pits."[26] When William Branson brought suit against Nutt's heirs in 1741, he owned: "and also of the moiety of an Iron mine with six acres of Land."

As mentioned, Branson obtained his share of the mine in 1725 from Nutt. Having already obtained the Nutt share, after Branson's death, Warwick partners Samuel Potts and Thomas Rutter obtained his portion from his heirs. They and their heirs maintained ownership until the entire tract was purchased by Hopewell Furnace owners, the E. & G. Brooke Company.

There is a partial *John Potts Rock Run Furnace Account Book* for the year 1743, at the Pennsylvania Archives that provides some insight into how the ore was mined. Debited to the Warwick Company, Potts employed two miners to dig the ore and several teamsters to haul the ore to Rock Run. John Caldwell, who was also paid for making hay, was paid for "24 Days Work at Minehole." John Glenney was paid for "one Month & 6 Days Work in the Mine hole on his own Diet 3"12" 0." Additionally, Jacob Chauff is listed as a "Minor." Apparently, Potts was using gunpowder to help extract the ore as relative Henry Hockley was paid for bringing powder several times: "Brought Powder for the Mine." Also included on the same page are payments for digging and hauling limestone for the furnace.[27]

The ore was broken up on iron plates and put through a grate before it was used in the furnace. An inventory taken at Warwick in 1741 shows: "A grate to pound mine with one plate on each side" and "Four small plates to pound mine on."[28]

Batchelder, who visited the area when writing her *Potts Memorial* in 1874, gives a description more than 150 years after the ore was discovered but still being mined:

> "The mines which supplied these works [French Creek Iron Works] are situated a few miles above, and consist of surface deposits of brown and other hemitite ores; they are worked in an open quarry over several acres, and by a shaft one hundred and eighty feet deep. This rich mineral deposit was partly included in the grant of eight hundred acres to Samuel Nutt in 1718, and of one thousand more in 1733."[29]

Nutt's selection for his iron ore tract proved fortuitous. The mine became the second largest producer of iron ore in Pennsylvania after Cornwall. Although the area was closed several times during its history, as extraction and pumping techniques improved, the deposit had several re-openings. There was still mining on the property in the 1920s, but it had stopped by MacEltree's 1934 work: "A quarter of a mile northeast of the [granite] quarry is an iron-ore mine no longer used. A high stack, visible for a long distance, marks the entrance to this mine, which was fifteen hundred feet deep. It is closed today..."[30]

## NUTT'S FIRST FORGE AT COVENTRY, 1718-1719

*"Samuel Nutt, Sr., who in the early documents is described as a weaver, began clearing the dense forests at Coventry for another bloomery, which was the beginning of the famous Coventry Iron Works."*

ARTHUR BINING, *PENNSYLVANIA IRON MANUFACTURER*

*"I was in hopes I should have seen thee at the Forge before this time."*

SAMUEL NUTT TO ISAAC TAYLOR, 1720

By 1718, Samuel Nutt had a tract of land with a good iron source on it in Nantmeal Township, Chester County. He needed to build an ironwork close to it to use its ore and a road to connect the two. Additionally, the site had to be built near a stream to power his bellows and waterwheels. Nutt located a suitable seat southeast of the ore tract in Coventry Township at the forks of the French Creek. It would include land on both sides of the creek. To that end, Nutt requested a warrant from the land office for 800 acres dated August 17th, 1718, and a warrant for Nutt was issued to Taylor by the Commissioners of Property on October 2, 1718:

"At the request of Samuel Nutt now of Chester County that we would Grant him to take up near the Branches of the ffrench Creek the quantity of Eight hundred acres of Land for which he agrees to pay to ye use of ye Trustees Eighty pounds money of Pensilvania for the whole, and the yearly quit rent of one Shilling Sterling for each hundred Acres. These are to Authorize and Require thee to Survey or cause to be Survey'd unto the said Samuel Nutt at or near the place aforesaid according to the method of ye Townships appointed, the said quantity of Eight hundred acres of Land, that has not been already survey'd nor appropriated nor is Seated by the Indians, and make returns thereof unto the Secretary's Office, which Survey in case the said Samuel fulfil the above agreement within 3 months after the Date hereof shall be valid, otherwise the same to be void as if it had never been made, or this Warrant ever Granted. Given under our hands and Seal of the Province of Philadelphia [?] ye 2nd day of Octr, Anno D'ni, 1718."[31]

The Board of Property minutes note the warrant: "Samuel Nut of Chester County, requests a Grant of 800 acres of Land back in said County, for which he is to pay £10 p. C't and one Shilling Sterling quitrent. A Warrant is threupon signed, dated 2, 8[mo,], 1718."[32] While the warrant called for 800 acres, only 300 were surveyed at that time. The survey at the land office that is connected to this property at the Archives states the following:

"The Draught of a Tract of Land in Coventry in the County of Chester containing three hundred acres surveyd for Samuel Nutt the 21th day of October 1720 in part of 800 acres granted to him (the said Samuel) by the Commissioners of Property in their Warrant dated the 2d day of October 1718 retuned into Secretarys Office the 16th day of August 1725 by Jacob Taylor.

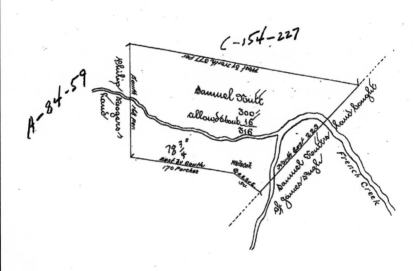

The Draught of a Tract of Land in Coventry in the County of Chester containing Three hundred acres surveyd for Samuel Foult the 21st day of October 1720 in part of 800 acres Granted to him (the said Samuel) by the Commissioners of Property in their Warrant Dated the the 2d day of October 1718 Returned into Secretarys Office the 16th day of August 1725 by

Jacob Taylor

*IN TESTIMONY that the above is a copy of the original remaining on file in the Department of Internal Affairs of Pennsylvania, made con-*

*Taylor 1720 Survey Attached to Warrant* [33]

Taylor also surveyed Philip Rogers' land which was west, but contiguous to Nutt's tract at the same time and both tracts are listed on the survey. Located southeast of the mine, Nutt's tract contained the forks of the North and South Branches of the French Creek. Nutt erected his bloomery on this property. It was close to the French Creek and located south of Route 23. Although he obtained partners fairly quickly, it is assumed he built his bloomery "on his own strength."

With the erection of Nutt's Bloomery, the iron industry in Chester County had begun. The exact date the ironwork began making iron is unknown. It had a very short existence and was replaced by a refinery forge, which became the well-known Coventry Forge. In 1941, the Chester County Historical Society put a granite marker to mark the spot of Nutt's first ironwork. The marker is located near French Creek in Warwick Park. It is simply engraved: "Coventry Forge 1717." A 1717 date seems early based on the warrant date of August 1718. Iron historian Arthur Bining gives 1718 as its starting date, and that has generally been used by later historians. But in 1719, Nutt was assessed in the "Skoolkill" district as a **non-resident** which meant he at the very least, did not winter over that year.[34] He is listed as a resident in 1720. In that same year, a contemporary account (the only one uncovered) notes the forge was in operation. Construction of the forge was probably started in 1718.

In July of 1718, Jonathan Dickinson writing from Philadlephia, states: "The expectations from the ironworks forty miles up the Schuylkill are very great."[35] Although he appears to have been discussing Rutter Bloomery in Philadelphia County, early iron historians probably based on the 1718 date of the Taylor letter and the 1717/1718 warrants Nutt filed, thought he was also talking about Nutt's endeavors.[36] This would have matched the time that Nutt went to the land office. This Dickinson's letter was similarly used to confirm the 1718 date that Nutt began producing iron. While he obviously could have been talking about both Rutter and Nutt, it is not until 1720 that we have confirmation that this forge was a going concern and he was producing iron.

Nutt's first ironwork had a short existence, lasting only for about four years. His forges and the furnaces would be built on this 300-acre

tract of land. Nutt retained full
ownership of this tract until 1724,
when he took 100 acres of the 300
acres and divided it by thirds, selling one-third each to his partners.
However, as with his ore tract, he
had not received his patent yet and
the sale was not recorded.

Nutt did not receive a patent
on the forge tract property until
June 8, 1736. The Commissioner's
Minutes of 11th 3mo 1736 list the
various patents:   "To Sam'l Nutt
for two Tracts in Chester County,
**300 Acres in Coventry**, 600 Acres
in Nantmell--959 by the Comm'rs      *Chester County Historical Society*
Warr't in 1717 at £10 @ C't & 1s      *Marker for Nutt's First Ironwork*
Sterl. quitr't."[37]

While Samuel Nutt was starting Chester County's iron industry,
he became involved in a court order. Chester County Orphan Court records of the twenty fourth day of February Anno Domi 1718, state that
Isaac Taylor, Ephraim Jackson and Samuel Nutt were appointed to audit
the account of William Bartram's estate taken by Stephen Jackson and
William Smith. They were to report their findings to the next Orphan's
Court.[38]

## FUTURE WARWICK FURNACE TRACT AT NANTMEAL AND LAND FOR COALING, 1718

Shortly after warranting the two tracts that contained his mine and
ironwork, Samuel Nutt began a twenty-year process of warranting large
tracts of land in Nantmeal and Coventry near the branches of French
Creek. At his death in 1737, he would own over 2,100 acres of land.
This land was needed for "coaling" for both his forge and later furance.

FORM No. 1.

Samuel Nutt's Land

C154-228

West 535 perches

Samuel Nutt 650 Acres
and allowance of Six ⅌ Cent

Nicholas Rogers

Henry Horkley

C-182-449

East 52 B. oak

North rd.

North 170

East 212 P⁵

Gum

White Oak

Wm Branson

South 112

N. East 182

N. 31d E. 81.P⁵

Black oak

Griffith Evan

Griffith Griffiths

In Pursuance of two Warrants from ye Comm'rs of Property, one
for 400 acres dated 18th of 7ᵇʳ 1717, The other for 800 acres dated the
2d of 8ᵇʳ 1718. Survey'd to Saml Nutt on the 27th May 1726, The above
Described Tract of Land. Situate in Coventrey—in Chester County
Containing Six Hundred & fifty Acres & the allowance of Six ⅌
Cent.

Jnº Taylor ——

IN TESTIMONY that the above is a copy of the original remaining on file in
the Department of Internal Affairs of Pennsylvania, made
conformably to an Act of Assembly approved the 16th day of
February, 1833, I have hereunto set my Hand and caused
the Seal of said Department to be affixed, at Harrisburg,
this twenty eighth day of April 1910.

Henry Houck

Secretary of Internal Affairs.

*Taylor Survey of 650-Acre Tract*[39]

Cold-blast furnaces particularly needed large amounts of charcoal and at its height, Warwick was using over an acre a day of trees when in blast.

On October 2, 1718, Samuel Nutt filed for his additional 650 acres. Having 150 acres left from the 400-acre warrant his ore tract was on, and 500 acres left from the 800-acre warrant his forge tract was on, they combined the two and Taylor surveyed a tract of 650 acres upstream from Coventry in Nantmeal Township. This land would eventually become the tract Warwick Furnace was built on in 1737. Taylor writes on the survey: "In Pursuance of two Warrants from ye Commrs of Property, one for 400 acres dated 18th of 7br 1717. The other for 800 acres dated the 2d of 8br 1718. Survey'd to Saml Nutt on the 27th May 1726." This land was located in Nantmeal Township.

# PARTNERSHIP AND SECOND COVENTRY FORGE, 1720-1724

*"We had a lott of men goeing upon making of Iron they are at work at the Blumorry wch doth not so well make Iron as a furnace would yet the Iron is generally approved in England wch hath been sent over and our smiths work up all the make & say it is as good as any of ye best Sweeds Iron."*

JONATHAN DICKINSON, DISCUSSING
RUTTER'S FORGE, 1719[40]

Like Thomas Rutter's bloomery, Nutt's first ironwork had a short existence and it was replaced fairly quickly by a refinery forge. In 1720, Samuel Nutt sent a letter to Isaac Taylor, indicating his first forge was operational, he probably had taken on partners by then and they intended on building a second ironwork in the fall.

"Philadelphia, July 2nd, 1720. My Good friend, I was in hopes I would have seen thee at the Forge before this time but suppose some other Important Affairs presented it - however I had not that happiness; I make Bold to trouble thee a few Lines; to acquaint that **Wee** proceed on; In **our** Intentions of putting up another forge this fall upon the french Creek a little above James Pughs upper line and shall Dam up above the forks of the North & South Branches so that **we** will be under an absolute necessity of taking up all that Tract that lies betwixt the said James Pughs line & Philip Rogers up the

North branch and although I do not think the land is invit-
ing to any other body to medle with it - yet if anyone should
attempt to do so: I desire thee to Interpose thy good offices
in **our** favour & in doing so thou will in a Particular manner
oblige thy sir to serve thee at all times."[41]

By July 1720, Nutt had a mine and was producing iron at Coventry. The fact that he uses "our" and "we" in his Taylor letter would
indicate that he was already or intended shortly to be in partnership with
William Branson and probably Mordecai Lincoln. With the additional
capital, he was planning or was already building a second forge.[42] Nutt
was also telling Taylor he intended to buy more land near the forge and
was asking him not to warrant any should someone apply until he had a
chance to file for it.

In 1719, Manatawny ironmaster Thomas Rutter, formed a company named Rutter, Coates and Company to capitalize the construction
of Colebrook Dale Furnace near modern-day Boyertown, which they
began building that year.[43] Colebrook Dale was Pennsylvania's first cold
blast furnace and was in blast the following year. Rutter converted his
bloomery forge to a refinery forge and began making iron through a
more efficient two-step process. Nutt would follow suit at Coventry by
obtaining partners and building his own furnace.

## PARTNERSHIP

Partnerships were common in the early colonial iron industry. Obtaining capital was a tricky business. The cost to purchase land and to
build a furnace at that time was considerable and the risk was substantial.
By bringing in partners, the expense and risk were shared. Of the first six
ironworks in Pennsylvania and Delaware as given by iron historian Arthur
Bining, two met with "indifferent success" and another "never prospered."
Consequently, considering the investment amount, obtaining the amount
of capital needed often required several investors. Nutt attracted William
Branson, a Philadelphia Quaker merchant to invest in the venture and

Mordecai Lincoln to help with the work at the furnace. Sometime in the early 1720s, they formed a company and built a second forge near the first but on higher ground. Nutt, the experienced ironmaster, brought vision and capital in the form of land and an ore mine that proved an excellent and continued source of iron. William Branson, the merchant, brought the capital needed for expansion and the business connections in Philadelphia. His store there also served as the initial outlet for the company's iron. Mordecai Lincoln, an "ironmonger," worked with Nutt at the forge. The second forge was built on this land on the south side of the road on the land that Lincoln was living on. The company lasted for four years.

## WILLIAM BRANSON

William Branson (1682-1760), Nutt's partner, was the son of Nathaniel and Mary (Bacon) Branson, Quakers of the Parish of Sonning, Berkshire, England. Sonning was about three miles from Reading, the largest town in Berkshire and a major iron-producing center in the 1700s. Branson, a Friend, immigrated to Philadelphia in 1708. His father had purchased 1,250 acres from William Penn that was in Brandywine Township and conveyed the land to William on August 28, 1707. William's father never emigrated. In 1709, Branson resided in Philadelphia on the east side of Second Street and in 1717, was noted as a "Joyner." He must have followed this trade for a number of years, for he is listed as a Freeman in the Minutes of the Common Council, having purchased his license to operate as an individual tradesman on May 20, 1717.[44]

In 1720, he is listed as a shopkeeper, in 1724, as a merchant, in 1740, as an ironmonger and by 1745 as a gentleman. Regardless of his vocation, he had excess capital to invest and he invested in the iron industry. His iron investments made him rich and by 1754, he paid the second highest tax in Philadelphia and is listed as a merchant. Branson became the financier for the various Coventry iron endeavors and his store in Philadelphia was a major outlet for the company's goods. He appears to also have been an investor in 1720 in Thomas Rutter's company, although perhaps not a major one. Articles of Agreement dated

January 14, 1722/23, also indicate he, and later Coventry partner, Jonathan Robeson, along with Thomas Shute and James Steel, opened an iron mine on Marcus Hulings' Amity tract near Rutter's ironwork.[45] As with Lincoln, it is unknown how Branson and Nutt met. The two remained partners after Lincoln left in 1724 and they invested with Jonathan Robeson in Coventry's first furnace. Branson would become a major purchaser of land in Chester County and he generally lists himself on deeds and agreements through the 1750s as a "merchant."

## MORDECAI LINCOLN

Mordecai Lincoln (1686-1736), Nutt and Branson's partner at Coventry, was the son of Mordecai Lincoln and the grandson of Samuel and Sarah (Jones) Lincoln, immigrants from Norfolk County, England. (He was Abraham Lincoln's great-great grandfather.) Samuel settled in Hingham, Massachusetts, where his fourth son, Mordecai was born in 1667. The elder Mordecai was a blacksmith and worked his trade at Hull. He moved to Scituate, Massachusetts, about 1704, where he established a furnace for the smelting of iron ore. His son, Mordecai, the Coventry ironmaster, was born in Hingham, Massachusetts, on April 24, 1686. With his brother Abraham, he migrated to Monmouth County, New Jersey, where he married Hannah Salter. He settled in Freehold, New Jersey, by 1714, and was living there when he removed to Chester County where he was living by 1720. He is listed on the first tax list for Chester County for 1720. How he and Nutt found each other is unknown but he brought skills in iron making to the partnership apparently acquired at his father's furnace. He lists himself in deeds and agreements as an "ironmonger." He lived at or near the forge as he and Nutt are shown on the 1720-1724 tax lists for Coventry.[46] In 1729, he married as his second wife, Mary Robeson, the daughter of Andrew Robeson and he disappears from Coventry tax records in that year.[47] On May 10th, 1732, Mordecai Lincoln, obtained from Thomas Millard, of Coventry, a conveyance of one thousand acres of land in Amity township, formerly belonging to Andrew Robeson. He lived there until his death in 1736.

*Lincoln Homestead Sign*

*Mordecai Lincoln House*

## SECOND FORGE AT COVENTRY, C.1722

*"Whereas They the said Samuel Nut William Branson and Mordecai Lincoln Have at their Joynt Charge lately Erected Built and provided one Dwelling House and a Forge with Engines belonging to their Iron Works besides other Buildings & Erections Situate Lying and being on a Certain Tract of Land at French Creek aforsd which Tract of Land is now in the Possession of the said Samuel Nut...by virtue of a Warrant from the Commissioners of Property dated the Eighteenth Day of September Anno Dom. 1717...."*

ARTICLES OF AGREEMENT DATED FEBRUARY 28, 1724[48]

Nutt and Lincoln were living at the bloomery forge by 1720 when they both appear on the first assessment of the district in Chester County of the inhabitants taken that year: "Near ye Branches of the ffrench Creek & ye Branches of Brandywine...Sam' Nutt, £20, Mordicay Lincoln £12." This was the first tax Nutt appeared on and neither he nor Lincoln are shown on the 1718 or 1719 tax lists as residents for the Skool Kill District which the forge location was originally in.

Several Lincoln family articles indicate about 1720, Lincoln warranted and lived on 150 acres of land near the forge. The property is noted as just west of Coventryville.[49] This appears incorrect. Without question, Lincoln was living on the western part of the company land and probably in the dwelling noted in records as located next to the forge. It is not known if he purchased the property, but the Articles of Agreement for the second forge recite a line running westerly by the: "Land of the above named Mordecai Lincoln." It appears to be the 1/3 of the 100 acres that Nutt sold to him in 1724. Lincoln moved back to New Jersey before Nutt obtained the patent in 1736 and consequently, the sale was not recorded.

In 1721, "Mordecaj Linerwood" was taxed £20. That same year, Nutt was assessed £50: "for all his land in this County." In 1722, Samuel Nutt in "Nantmel," was assessed for "the forge" which was valued at £20.

In 1724, only "The Forge" is listed. As indicated, Nutt's initial forge lasted four years when it was replaced by a refinery forge. Its exact erection date is unknown but it would appear that the three partners built the second forge without a formal agreement probably in 1722.

On May 23, 1721, Nutt had purchased from James Peugh (Pugh) 300 acres, part of 700 acres Pugh had warranted on the French Creek, in Coventry which was southeast and adjacent to Nutt's original forge land. Pugh had received a patent on the property on Novmber 4, 1713. Using three acres (sometimes six are indicated) of the Pugh property, Nutt took 97 acres of the 300-acre Coventry tract and created a 100-acre parcel. This 100 acres was called in various documents "the company land"and it was bisected by what became Ridge Road. On the 100 acres, Nutt built a dam on the north branch of French Creek and a race to the forge to supply water to power the hammer. (Thomas Potts, owner of Coventry at that time, rebuilt the forge race in 1787.)

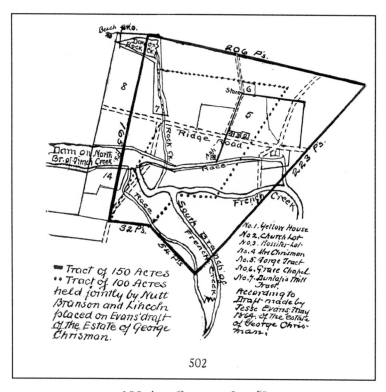

*100-Acre Company Land[50]*

Toward the end of 1723, Nutt split the company land into thirds. Articles of Agreement were signed on February 28, 1724, by Nutt and his partners.[51] They were witnessed by Henry Sutton and George Dandesson.[52] In that document, Nutt agreed to sell one-third of 100 acres of land including the buildings and erections aforesaid to Lincoln and Branson. However, at that time, Nutt had not received title to the tract yet from the Penn government and the document stated his intention of doing so. The Articles lay out the metes and bounds for 150 acres and then because it was the "intention and agreement of the sd Parties To Hold one Hundred Acres," laid out a sub-set of 97 acres. The MacEltree map on the previous page shows the 150- and 100-acre tracts.

The Articles indicate that the partners had: "lately Erected Built and provided one Dwelling House and a Forge with Engines belonging to their Iron Works besides other Buildings & Erections Situate Lying and being on a Certain Tract of Land at French Creek." This forge became the well-known Coventry Forge and had a long life span. It outlasted all the other ironworks that Nutt would build.

Signed on the same day as the Articles of Agreement, were two Obligations. The first was between William Branson, Merchant of Philadelphia, and Nutt for £1,000. It appears to be simply capital for the ironwork. The second was between Samuel Nutt of Coventry upon the French Creek, Ironmonger and Mordecai Lincoln of the same place, Ironmonger, by which Lincoln contributed three-hundred pounds lawful money of Pennsylvania for one-third of six acres of a 250-acre tract that was deemed to be one-half of the iron mine. The agreement noted that Nutt had received a patent on the property on August 20, 1718.[53]

As indicated, both Nutt and Lincoln were living at or near the forge by 1720. A "dwelling" was built on Lincoln's portion near the forge and Nutt was living in the eastern part in a house on the north side of the road. Morris indicates the earliest part of the house Nutt was living in by the 1730s dates from 1719, but its date of construction is a guess. Nutt's 1720 letter to Isaac Taylor indicates a second forge would be built in the fall of 1720 and Lincoln's Articles of Agreement confirm that it was built at French Creek and was active by 1724.

It was this second forge, called the French Creek Iron Forge when the furnace closed, that became the well-known Coventry Forge and it remained in production well into the 1800s. This forge is mentioned in Samuel Nutt's estate accounting dated May 1738 under the column listing what he owned jointly with William Branson: "250 acres of land with the forge, dwelling and sundry out houses erected thereon." It is thought the first forge was built too close to French Creek so this forge was built on higher ground to avoid flooding.

Because the second forge remained active and in existence until the 1800s, of all Nutt's five ironworks at Coventry, this location is the best known. Frederick Sheeder (1777-1865), in his East Vincent Township history written in 1845, states: "Samuel Nutt erected the first iron works along french creek above george Christman's dam in Covantry."[54] Cremers indicates the second forge was moved to the corner of Coventryville Road and Route 23. In 1874, Mrs. Batchelder went to find Nutt's early works but by then, any remains of Coventry Forge was gone: "Those in operation there about 1734 were, as far as I can learn, Redding Furnace, Coventry Forge, and the Vincent Steel-Works; though the place once occupied by the last two has been pointed out to me, I was unable to trace any remains of the buildings that once stood there."[55]

It is presumed that the inital forge was probably closed after the new one began production as the tax records for Chester County in 1722 and 1724 only mention one forge. Nutt was assessed for the forge 1722 in Nantmeal and 1724 in Coventry. Although the physical remains of both these forges had long since disappeared, MacEltree tried to place both their locations:

> "The exact site of Old Coventry Forge is hard to determine. After an examination of draughts, courses of various roads, location of the breast of another dam and other markers, I am inclined to believe that the original Forge [bloomery] was about 450 feet southwest of the marker and the later forge [finery] about 250 feet southeast of the marker. My views harmonize with those of William L. Christman, Esq., the present owner of the premises. He informs me that there is evidence that the coal house of the old forge stood a

few yards west of the road leading south to Nantmeal where the abandoned right of way of the Delaware River and Lancaster Railroad a bridge about a hundred feet north of this spot which was then supposed to be all that was left of the tail race of the original forge."[56]

The marker noted by MacEltree, was erected by the Chester County Historical Society on Ridge Road (Route 23) in Coventryville in 1910. MacEltree put a facsimile in his 1936 book. Cyrus T. Fox in a *Reading Eagle* article dated February 7, 1916, from his series on the early iron industry, also notes the marker: "It is so placed as to point in the direction of an ash in the meadow through which the south branch of the French Creek flows."

*1910 Chester County Historical Society Marker*[57]

## SAMUEL NUTT, 1720-1726

In addition to his ironwork endeavors, Samuel Nutt was involved in a number of other business and public activities. To support and eventually expand his iron business, he continued to acquire land through purchase and through warrant from the Penn government. For the most part, the warranted land was heavily forested and near his works and would be used for charcoal. The already mentioned tract of 650 acres on French Creek, including the subsequent site of Warwick Furnace, was surveyed to him May 2, 1719, in Nantmeal, and 150 acres more on October 21, 1720.[58] In 1723, in addition to running the forges, Samuel Nutt was elected as a member of the Assembly from Chester County.[59] He was elected for a second time in 1726.[60] Additionally, he was appointed as one of the justices of Chester County in 1724, and again on August 25, 1726.[61]

In 1720, Thomas Rutter's son-in-law, Samuel Savage, died near Rutter's Bloomery on his tract of land in Amity. Savage's will dated September 25, 1719, was filed at Philadelphia. On July 16, 1720, Samuel Nutt and Francis Purnill appraised his estate. Anna (Rutter) Savage was named sole executrix. Samuel and Anna would marry six years later.

Things were changing across the river at the Rutter Works. On January 13, 1725, Thomas Rutter reorganized his company and rented his ironworks to a number of investors for a term of 28 years for £30 per year. Thomas Potts, a Germantown butcher, rented the works from the other investors and with his 15-year-old son, John, moved to Colebrook Dale Furnace where he would eventually become its ironmaster. Thomas Potts would play a major role in the development of the Pennsylvania iron industry. Rutter did it first, but Potts would do it better. Potts brought management skills and organization to the new industry and eventually developed a nascent production and distribution system. He also implemented a multi-furnace, multi-forge concept that his son, John, who founded Pottstown, would enhance. As part of the 1725 reorganization, Thomas Rutter moved to Rutter's Forge in Amity Township and ran it for the new company.

As indicated, on December 14, 1725, along with a description of what the company built, Mordecai Lincoln sold his one-third share of the company to William Branson. The document was "Signed, sealed and delivered in the presence of Jno. Robeson and Jane Speary":

"Know all men by these Pres[ts] that I Mordecai Lincoln of Coventry In the County of Chester, for and in Consideration of the Sum of Five Hundred Pounds of Currant Lawful Money of America...for Ever quit claim unto him the said William Branson his Heirs and Assigns for Ever...the one full undivided third Part of one Hundred Acres of Land... [and] six Acres of Land...Together with all and Singular of the Mynes and Minerals Forges Building, Houses Lands Improvements whatsoever thereunto belonging...”[62]

When Branson purchased the land from Lincoln, Nutt was still ten years away from obtaining the patent from the Penns, so it could not be legally transferred. (It appears from the *Letters of Attorney* documents that Nutt was in no apparent hurry to obtain complete title to much of his land.) Branson inserted the following language into the document:

“[the] Parcel of Land Surveyed & Returned to the said Samuel Nutt being that same Tract as was lately in possession and occupation of Mordecai Lincoln which said Land by reason of the Land Office being Shut up a full & absolute Title cannot be procured by the sd Sam[ll] Nutt from the proprietor. Now the true Condition Intent & meaning of these Presents are That the Sd Samuel Nutt shall immediately after the opening of the said Office (or as soon as a good Sufficient Title can be procured from the Proprietor) He the said Samuel Nutt shall purches or Procure the same...shall make over and Convey to the Said William Branson.”[63]

Although not serving in the Assembly in 1725, Nutt was “undoubtedly one of the signers” of a “Petition of some Persons concerned in the Iron-Works, setting forth, the pernicious Effects of selling Liquors near those Works” that year. The petition, “praying Leave to bring in a Bill to prohibit same, and that the Selling of Rum, and other Spirits, by Permits, be wholly prohibited.”[64] By limiting distribution sites, the ironmasters were trying to control the sale of liquor to their workforce. The petition led to the passage of a law in February of 1736, to regulate retailers of liquors near the ironworks, which gave the ironmasters both the ability to veto tavern permits and a monopoly for the distribution of liquor to their workforce.[65]

On May 12, 1725, Samuel Nutt was appointed a Justice of the Peace for Chester County. He was reappointed August 26, 1726, October 19, 1727, and August 25, 1729. He was not appointed in 1730.[66]

On April 29, 1725, Samuel Nutt, of the Township of Coventry in Chester County, ironmonger, and his wife, Anna, sold to John Henderson, of the County of Philadelphia, 425 acres of land in Sadsbury Township that he had purchased in England prior to immigrating for £90.[67] Six months later, Samuel Nutt, ironmonger, of Chester County, was one of eight individuals, including William Branson and Thomas and John Rutter, who on October 15, 1725, formed a company with Samuel James as the head, for the purpose of building Abington Furnace in New Castle County, Delaware, on Christiana Creek. They purchased 1,000 acres and built a forge and furnace called the Abington Iron Works. This venture unfortunately did not prosper.[68] It was apparently still active on July 30, 1741. It is noted in a *Pennsylvania Gazette* article of that date concerning the estate of Samuel James when it was listed as the furnace commonly known as "Samuel James' or Abington."

About this time, sometime prior to the April 1725 indenture noting the sale of his 425-acre Sadsbury land on which she is mentioned, Samuel Nutt married Samuel Savage's widow, Anna (Rutter) Savage, the daughter of Thomas Rutter. Their exact date of marriage or where they were married has not been discovered. Nutt was aged 50 years and Anna was 39. Marrying into the large Rutter family would involve Nutt in a number of family transactions including wills and land dealings.

## ANNA (RUTTER) SAVAGE

Anna Rutter (1686-1745) was the oldest child of pioneer ironmaster, Thomas Rutter and his wife, Rebecca Staples. She was born in Germantown on the "25th of ye 8mo 1686." She married Samuel Savage, a stonemason, about 1704. Savage probably helped build Rutter's Bloomery, Rutter's Forge and Colebrook Dale Furnace. They had six children, five of whom lived to adulthood (Samuel, Thomas, Joseph, Ruth and Rebecca). In 1716, the family moved to Amity Township near Rutter's ironworks in the Manatawny Region where Samuel purchased 800 acres of land. Savage died in 1720. Anna married Samuel Nutt probably in 1725 and moved to Coventry with her five children, the oldest of whom was fifteen. Due to the untimely deaths of her husband, her son-in-law and son, Anna Nutt would end up running Warwick Furnace, probably making her the first woman industrialist in America.

Anna (Rutter) Savage Nutt's five children would play an important role in the Nutt iron empire. Her three sons, Samuel, Thomas and Joseph, as they grew, were trained at Coventry in iron making and Samuel was actively involved in iron making. Her two daughters married ironmasters. The oldest daughter, Ruth, married John Potts, the son of Colebrook Dale ironmaster, Thomas Potts. Her second daughter, Rebecca, married Nutt's heir and nephew, Samuel Nutt Jr.[69] Samuel and Anna (Rutter) Nutt remained married for 14 years until Nutt's death.

After their marriage, Samuel and Anna lived in what has been called Coventry Hall. It was located north of the road across from the forge and is no longer standing.[70] Cremers indicates that it was built c.1725 although Eleanor Morris says 1719. Nutt's estate accounting notes: "287 acres land in Coventry being the land on which Samuel Nutts house stands £300." Batchelder in her *Potts Memorial* provides the following:

> "The first house built by Samuel Nutt at Coventry, and where probably both Rebecca and Ruth Savage were married, has long since been taken down, but it was described to me (by an elderly lady still living, whose husband, much older than herself, lived in the neighborhood and remembered it well) as similar to the ancient houses in the old English town of Coventry. The frame was of immense hewn logs, between which were cemented stones; it was built be-

yond the present mansion house, and higher up the hill, and was standing until after the Revolution; for during that time Mrs. Grace (formerly Mrs. Nutt Jr.) entertained there the officers of Revolution."[71]

Estelle Cremers states:

> "This would have been a half-timber style with their great squared logs and their braced frame showing on the outside. By the inventory of the Nutts and Later Thomas Potts, it had four rooms per floor, probably divided by a central hall. It was remembered by an elderly Birmingham lady as having an iron plate on a gable that read 'S.Nutt,' and is thought to have stood into 1850 or lter."[72]

## RUTTER FAMILY

Samuel Nutt's marriage to Thomas Rutter's oldest daughter made him a part of the large and influential Rutter family. Nutt went from having no relatives to having a number of them. He became involved in their various legal and domestic affairs during the ensuing decade, signing several legal documents for various transactions and serving as an executor for the estates of Anna's two brothers and as trustee for Thomas Rutter. About the time of Nutt's marriage, his father-in-law had rented out Colebrook Dale Furnace and moved to his forge in Amity Township northwest of what is now Pottstown.[73]  Thomas Potts began running Colebrook Dale Furnace and would replace Rutter as the preeminent ironmaster of Pennsylvania.[74]

# 1770 MAP BY WILLIAM SCULL SHOWING COVENTRY, WARWICK AND READING

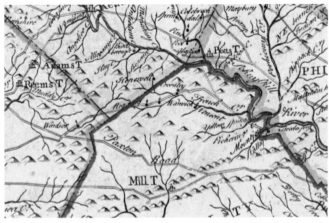

*Courtesy of Library of Congress*

*"To the Honorable Thomas Penn and Richard Penn, Esquires, true and absolute proprietaries and Governors of the Province of Pennsylvania and the territories thereunto belonging and to the Honorable John Penn, Esquire, Lieutenant-Governor of the same, this map. Of the Province of Pennsylvania."*

1770

# PART II

## FRENCH CREEK IRON-WORKS, 1726-1738

*Eighteenth Century Six Plate Stove side plate cast at Warwick Furnace by Rutter & Potts. Courtesy of The Jacob Brothers Collection.*

# FIRST FURNACE
# ON ROCK RUN,
# 1726

*"The Petition of Samuel Nutt, William Branson and Jonathan Robeson Humbly Shewth That Whereas ye Petitioners haveing Laid out great sums of money To building and Errecting of Iron works for the making of Iron In this Country..."*

1726 ROAD PETITION

*"A furnace erects its own monument, the slag or cinder is as durable as granite, and would hold its own even against written records."*

ISAAC W. VAN LEER

Between Mordecai Lincoln's sale of his share of the forge and property in December 1725, and an Obligation from Samuel Nutt to William Branson in December of 1726, a new partnership was formed and the new company built a cold blast furnace on Rock Run. Called in contemporary accounts: "the Furnace at Rock Creek," it was built on the west bank near where Rock Run enters French Creek. It was on land previously inhabited by Lincoln on the same parcel as the refinery forge. Lincoln apparently owned the western half of Nutt's 300-acre forge tract.

The 1726 Obligation shows without doubt, the partners built the furnace:

41

"The said William Branson, together with the said
Samuel Nutt and Jonathan Robeson have Built & Erected a
ffurnace for the Running and Melting of Iron on a branch of
the Creek commonly called French Creek in the said Township of Coventry upon a Piece or Parcel of Land Surveyed &
Returned to the said Samuel Nutt."

There has been considerable confusion of the name of this furnace.
The new furnace was called Redding #1 in secondary accounts and by
Henry Mercer as Christine.[75] It produced iron for over 10 years and was
replaced or rebuilt in 1736 by a newer furnace later named Rock Run
Furnace. Its location is given in the Obligation as built on: "that same
Tract as was lately in the possession and occupation of Mordecai Lincoln
which said land by reason of the Land Office being Shut up a full &
absolute Title cannot be procured by the sd Sam[ll] Nutt from the proprietor."[76] In effect, by 1726, Nutt still did not have title to the land and
apparently could not sell any of it to Lincoln. In a deed dated January 10,
1788, from the executors of John Potts to his eldest son, Thomas Potts
(Nutt's step-son-in-law), "Samuel Nutt's siesin of three hundred acres is
recited and also his conveyance to William Branson of a moiety of two
hunderd and fifty acres: "whereon Coventry Forge and the old Furnace
formerly stood."[77]

Cremers notes its location: "The old Rock Run Furnace building
(ca 1720) and Coventry Iron Works had disappeared by the end of the
19th century. The position of the furnace, however, is clearly found by
charcoal that can be dug with little effort in the grassy bank between the
white house nearest the bridge on Mt. Pleasant Road and old Ridge Road
and the stone mill building behind it."[78]

Rachael Jones, the wife of William Jones, Branson's Reading Furnace's first manager, in an affidavit dated August 12, 1806, dates the
furnace as built c.1724/1725:

"Rachael Jones, who on her Solomn affirmation doth
Depose and say that she is now in her Ninety first year of age
and she sayeth that she remembers the building of the Fur-

nace on Rock Run was Built when she was in her tenth year of age and it always went by the name of Branson and Nutts Iron Works. The Forge was Built before her memory..."[79]

William Branson seemed to put up most of the capital needed to build it. The Obligation of Samuel Nutt to William Branson, Merchant, dated December 13, 1725, shows Branson provided £2,000 money of Pennsylvania for construction. The obligation gave Branson: "one third Part and one Tweleth part of all the said Land Together with the furnis & all Toolls belonging to the same & also all Buildings & Improvements unpone the Premisses...all pigmetle Cast at the sd Furnis." He was also to be charged appropriately for "Cole Ore Labour &ct that shall be wanting to Carry on the sd Iron Works."[80]

The new furnace partner was Jonathan Robeson. Jonathan Robeson fairly quickly left the partnership, but the date is unknown. At Nutt's death in 1738, Nutt and Branson each owned fifty percent of the works. Robeson must have left on good terms as Nutt's 1737 will names him as "a trusty and well-beloved friend."

## JONATHAN ROBESON

Jonathan Robeson (1690-1766), Samuel Nutt and William Branson's partner at the first furnace on Rock Run, was the fourth child of Andrew Robeson. His involvement with Nutt and Branson seems to be short lived and the exact date he left the company is unknown. Andrew Robeson, a Scottish immigrant, came to America about 1676 and settled in Glouschester, West New Jersey. Jonathan was born in Glouchester about 1690. His father moved to the Manatawny Region and purchased a large tract of land. At his father's death in 1720, Jonathan was left his father's estate there along with 1,000 acres of land. Robeson was a Friend and in 1721, Jonathan Robeson of the Township of Amity married Elizabeth Morris at Radnor Monthly Meeting. Samuel Nutt signed the marriage certificate. In 1723 Robeson was one of five individuals who laid out the road from Thomas Rutter's Colebrook Dale to Germantown so that Rutter could get his iron to Philadelphia. He was also an investor that year with William Branson and several others in an iron mine near Rutter's ironwork. He was one of the two witnesses who signed the 1725 agreement when Mordecai Lincoln sold his share of the forge to William Branson. Jonathan became Lincoln's brother-in-law in 1729 when Lincoln married Mary Robeson as his second wife. Robeson removed to Warren County, New Jersey, in 1740 and built Oxford Furnace there in 1741 with Joseph Shippen.[81]

The three partners sent a petition to build a road from their new furnace, which was laid out in 1726:

> "To His Majesties Justices of the Peace for the County of Chester at Their Court of quarter Sessions held for the sd County. The Petition of Samuel Nutt, William Branson and Jonathan Robeson Humbly Shewth  That Whereas ye Petitioners haveing Laid out great sums of money To building and Errecting of Iron works for the making of Iron In this Country which said manufacturing must unavoidably advance the intrest of the same  - But Ye Petitioners are very much Incomoded and the County Reduced to very great Dificulties and Dangers with Cattle and Horses In bringing Iron from the said works to the several parts of this County by Reason thereof as yet no Road laid out to the said works from any Part Thereof-Your Petitioners Therefore Humbly pray that some persons of good Judgement many be appointed to Lay out a Road from The said works to yough Land Meeting house which will in a great measure Remove the Dificulties Complained of and the petitione shall Ever pray &c."[82]

Robeson eventually left the partnership but the date is unknown. In 1736, the furnace was rebuilt or replaced by a newer one, also on Rock Run. Early researchers knew that there was a furnace involved with the forge at Coventry, but they didn't know anything about its history. Due to the confusion of this furnace's replacement and the later Reading Furnace built by William Branson, it was assigned the generic name Reading #1 in secondary sources. This was also the name given to the second furnace which was thought to be located in the same place. This second furnace was called Rock Run Furnace by 1743, when John Potts was running it.[83]

Regardless of the naming confusion, by 1726, there was an ore mine, dams and races, a cold blast furnace and a refinery forge near the confluence of the French Creek's two branches. Under the partnership of Nutt and Branson, the French Creek Iron-Works was created and began making and refining iron.

Nicholas Scull's 1756 map entitled "To the Honourable Thomas Penn and Richard Penn, Esqrs., true & absolute proprietaries & Governours of the Province of Pennsylvania & counties of New-Castle, Kent and Sussex on Delaware this map of the improved part of the Province of Pennsylvania," is the first to show the location of Warwick, Reading and Coventry Forge (shown as "Robert Grace" who owned it at that time). Hockley's Mill is also shown located east of Warwick on French Creek.

*Early Map Showing Coventry Forge*[84]

# FRENCH CREEK
# IRON-WORKS,
# 1726-1736

*"Aliud majus ad fluvium Schulkill extruetum
Dni Samuel Nuts, cum fornace & focis ferrariis."*
EMANUEL SWEDENBORG, 1736

## NUTT DEVELOPS A PRODUCTION SYSTEM

Building the furnace on Rock Run gave the partners the ability to produce iron at a much higher rate than by Nutt's Bloomery. The second Coventy Forge was, or was converted to, a refinery forge and the furnace/forge combination became known as the French Creek Iron-Works.[85] This name was used until after Nutt died and until the Rock Run Furnace was closed after Warwick Furnace was built. In later secondary accounts, the entire industry was just called Coventry. Robeson left the firm but the French Creek Iron-Works operated successfully until Nutt's death. Acrelius indicates that: "Nutt supplies four forges besides his own in Chester County."

The works were in operation by 1726, when Quaker minister Thomas Chalkley visited them. His journal entry for the fourth month of that year states: "On my return homewards I crossed the Schuylkill, and went to Samuel Nutt's iron-works, where I had a large, quite, solid meeting."[86] In the Spring of 1737, another Quaker minister, John Churchman, mentions the ironworks: "Towards the last of the third month I went to Sadsbury to settle a dispute about the bounds of land; and having something to do near Samuel Nutt's iron works on French Creek..."[87] Although the complex was called in original documents and in newspaper advertisements by Nutt the "French Creek Iron-Works," they are also listed by others in other contemporary documents as "Samuel Nutt's Iron Works," and later, the "Coventry Iron Works."

In addition to making pig iron at his furnace, Nutt was making castings and stove plates that were assembled into stoves. While his 1737 estate accounting lists both back plates and stove plates, no stove plates are known to exist with Nutt's name on them.[88] Rutter's Colebrook Dale Furnace was making stove plates as early as 1724, about the time that Nutt's furnace was completed. Mercer indicates that stoves were being produced by 1728 at Nutt and Branson's works.[89] These stoves were probably sold at Branson's store in Philadelphia. In 1739, Branson advertised in *Sower's Almanac* of that year that if perchance one of his plates should crack, "as indeed an all too sudden fire will crack the best stoves if they are cold," he would replace it with a new one.

The "French-Creek Iron Works" are mentioned in the September 16, 1731, *American Weekly Mercury* concerning William Branson's wagon that overturned while coming from the works on the way to Philadelphia. The wagon was "loaden with sixteen Hundred Weight of Iron." The article shows how remote the works were at the time. The driver lay for two days with "all the Iron upon him" before he was found. The same paper shows that the products the partners were making were being sold at William Branson's store in Philadelphia: "Very good Iron Pots and Kettles, fine and light, made and sold, by William Branson, in High-street, (or Market-street) opposite to the Bishops Shambles, at Three Pence per Pound."

"Mr. Samuel Nut's Iron-works" are mentioned in the November 7, 1735, *Mercury* concerning a lost hound. Additionally, a tract of land in Chester County was advertised for sale in the April 22, 1731, *Mercury* "Six Miles of Samuel Nutt's Iron Works" and as indicated, Quaker John Churchman refers to them in his journal in the Spring of 1737 and again in 1748, noting a "meeting at Henry Hockley's, near French Creek Iron works..."

The French Creek Iron-Works received worldwide recognition in 1736. In that year, Emanuel Swedenborg, Swedish theologian, scientist and philosopher, published a three-volume set in Latin on mineral extraction and copper and iron smelting around the world. In his chapter on iron production in Maryland and Pennsylvania, he notes Rutter's works and also indicates: "A works was built on the Schuylkill River by Master Samuel Nut, with hearth furnace and forges."[90]

Of interest, Swedenborg's publication is credited with helping to alert English ironmasters about the growing American iron industry and developing an awareness that Rutter and Nutt's ironworks were a threat to them, particularly the refining forges. In 1736, the Merchants and Ironmongers sent a petition to the House of Commons expressing their concerns: "The inhabitants of the British Colonies having already erected several Furnaces and Forges for the making of Bar Iron...they will be induced to work up the said Iron themselves, to the great Decay and Prejudice of the Iron Trade in this Kingdom."[91]

## SAMUEL NUTT, 1726-1730

In 1726, Samuel James, a millwright, spearheaded a company of investors who capitalized the building of Abington Furnace in New Castle County, Delaware, on the south bank of Christiana Creek. James owned the land and he or his son had built a forge on it about 1723. Both Samuel Nutt and William Branson invested in this venture and became partners along with Thomas and John Rutter. Initially having eight investors, shares were quickly divided. Later investors included: Reese Jones, Evan Owen, Caspar Wistar, John Leacock, William Fishbourne, Edward Bradley and William Monningham.[92] Nutt is listed on the deed as an ironmonger and Branson as a merchant. It was named Abington, perhaps because one of the investors had joined Abington Meeting that year. The Abington Iron-works had a checkered history and apparently were not a financial success. They closed about 1737. Nutt's investment is not mentioned in in his estate accounting.

Although Quaker minister Thomas Chalkley visited his works in 1726, Nutt's religious affiliation at that time is unknown. He was a Friend at immigration, but his distance from any established meeting negated his regular attendance. His wife's father, Thomas Rutter, who was also originally a Friend, was a Seventh Day Baptist minister at the time of Nutt's marriage. Several sources connect Nutt with the English Seventh Day Baptist Meeting at Nantmeal, which was established in 1726, when a number of parishioners left the Great Valley Church over which day of the week the Sabbath fell on. The church edifice was built in the first half of the 18th century and is generally referred to by writers by the name of French Creek Seventh Day Baptist Meeting. Although he provides no primary evidence, Charles H. Green in his biography on Nutt, states unequivocally that Sanuel Nutt became a member of this meeting. Albert Rogers also mentions Samuel Nutt (but only as an English resident near the meeting) in his discussion of the English Seventh Day Baptist Meeting at Nantmeal. Rogers does note in the chapter on "Nantmeal Revival" that the meeting was increased by converts from the Quakers.[93]

In 1726, Samuel Nutt was named one of the executors of the will of George Carter of Bradford Township. Samuel would serve as executor of several individuals during his lifetime. On May 11, 1728, Nutt wrote a much copied letter from "Malanton." (This was an early name for Amity Township specifically located where Douglassville is now and near Thomas Rutter's forge.) Samuel Nutt wrote Governor Patrick Gordon about a "melancholy" incident concerning the murder of three Native Americans:

"May it please the Governour : —

Just now I R'ved the Disagreeable news that one Walter Winter & John Winter, e&., have Murdered one Indian Man & Two Indian Women, without any cause given by the sd Indians, & the sd Winter's have brought 2 girls (one of which is Cripled) to Geo. Boon's to receive some Reward. I desire the Governour may see after it before he goes Down; for most Certainly such actions will create the greatest antipathy betwix the Several nations of Indians & the Christians. The bearer, John Petty has heard the full Relation of this Matter; to whom I shall Refer the Governour for a more full account & Remain the Governour's most hearty friend and Serv't to Command."[94]

In February 1729, Samuel Nutt was one of 12 honest men appointed to a commission by Governor Patrick Gordon to fix the boundaries for a new county which was to be called Lancaster. The governer was reacting to a petition of the Chester County settlers on Octororo Creek. Nutt was no longer in the Assembly, but he perhaps still owned land in Sadsbury Township near what would become the border. The commissioners met with surveyor John Taylor and submitted a report in May of 1729. Nutt was the only commissioner whose name did not appear on the return of the survey of the new county line indicating that perhaps he did not participate.[95]

Samuel Nutt was elected as the commissioner from Chester County in 1730. Three commissioners were elected or appointed yearly, one from each of the three Pennsylvania counties then in existence. Commissioners were required to issue precepts to the constables, requiring them to make returns to the assessors of the names and estates of the inhabitants, and the assessors were required to lay the rates thereon.[96]

While Nutt was assisting in a number of "publick duties," William Branson also was involved in several. William Branson was part of a meeting in Philadelphia in 1729, called to fix the value of European currency used in the colony.[97]

Pioneer Ironmaster Thomas Rutter, died in 1730 and the *Pennsylvania Gazette* dated March 5 to March 19, 1729-30, records Rutter's death: "On Sunday night last died here Thomas Rutter, Sen., of short illness. He was the first that erected an ironwork in Pennsylvania." Rutter's wife, Rebecca was named "Whole and Sole Executrix" of the 1729 will but Rutter appointed his two sons-in-law, Samuel Nutt and Joseph Hall, Trustees, to see his testament performed and to assist Rebecca. Nutt was left a bequest in the will of 19 pounds.

## THE PENNSYLVANIA MARKET

In 1727, Pennsylvania's third cold-blast furnace was built. In that year, the Durham Furnace Company was formed and they built a cold-blast furnace near the Delaware River in what is now Durham Township,

Bucks County. It went into blast in 1728. Up until that time, the Rutter and Nutt companies had a monopoly on iron production and distribution to Philadelphia. The new furnace did not appear to change that. Durham was built with the intention of sending its pig iron to England and its output did not compete with Nutt's in the Pennsylvania market. Initially, they didn't even build a forge to refine the pig iron. Perhaps because of Branson's Philadelphia connections and his store there that served as an immediate outlet, Nutt (and Rutter) realized that Pennsylvania iron could be used in Pennsylvania. Almost from the outset, Pennsylvania furnaces had a higher ratio of forges to furnaces than Maryland or Virginia to refine its iron to be used locally. They did not need English markets or the ironmasters there to refine their iron. Pennsylvania iron could remain in Pennsylvania; something both the American ironmasters came to understand and the English ironmasters came to fear.

## ROADS TO AND FROM THE FRENCH CREEK IRON-WORKS—A DISTRIBUTION SYSTEM

When the French Creek Iron-Works were built, transportation in the areas outside of Philadelphia was in its nascent state and the area was at best isolated. Nutt could make as much iron as he wanted at Coventry, but unless he could get it to market, which in this case was Philadelphia, his efforts to create a succcessful business were doomed to failure. Nutt needed roads to transport his iron to Philadelphia. The first road return as a result of an Order of Court held at Chester dated August, 1725, shows how remote the French Creek Works were. The road was laid out from Moore Hall on Pickering Creek towards Philadelphia and the return mentions: "the path leading to the forge."[98] In 1726, when Nutt, Branson and Robeson petitioned the Justices of Chester County, there was no road yet to Coventry:

> "But Ye Petitioners are very much Incomoded and the County Reduced to very great Dificulties and Dangers with Cattle and Horses In bringing Iron from the said works to

the several parts of this County by Reason thereof as yet no Road laid out to the said works from any Part Thereof."

The petition was reviewed at the court session held on November 29, 1726. This road was laid out and the return filed the 24th of Feb. 1726/27. Although adjusted several times, it eventually became known as "Nutt's Road" and is listed as such in numerous early deeds and road petitions. The road went from the ironworks east ending at the Schuylkill River at the future site of Valley Forge. It is noted as laid out from "the iron-works on the St. Vincent river in the township of Coventry in County of Chester leading to Uwchlan meeting house" beginning at the forge at the distance of four miles passing over "Mt. Austrie."[99]

Cremers discusses Nutt's Road:

"Route 23 was built by Coventry ironmaster, Samuel Nutt, to transport iron to Moore's Landing at the mouth of Pickering Creek, where it could be rafted to Philadelphia, or could connect with other roads into the city and outlying villages. Nutt had several choices for eastern delivery. He could send his iron north over the Chestnut Hills to Potts' Landing on the Schuylkill, the nearest landing, but a hard pull for his teams when loaded with heavy iron. It was easier to send it by team roughly along French Creek, a generally downhill trail, to the river at Moore's, and later a shorter distance to Parker's Landing. The trail to Moore's mill is still known as Nutt's Road through Phoenixville. Later, Route 23 became a cattle drover's road."[100]

Chester County historian, Miriam Clegg, also mentions Nutt's Road: "Nutt saw a way to make a short cut in his journey [on Nutt's Road to Philadelphia] by relocating a section of road so that it ran straight through from the French Creek crossing to Corner Stores, and thence to Valley Forge. He persuaded the county road jury to make this change in 1735."[101] In that same year, at the February 1735 Court of Quarter Sessions for Lancaster County, the court received a petition for a road in

Caernarvon Township from "Nathan Evans' Mill by the new Church, extending through Chester County to Samuel Nutt's forge."[102]

In 1736, the Court of Quarter Sessions received a petition from "most of the blacksmiths of Lancaster County who deal at Samuel Nutt's" for their iron to build a road from the Coventry Works to Lancaster.[103] The Minutes of the Board of Property for January 4th, 1738, indicate that a petition of sundry inhabitants of the county of Lancaster was read before the Board of Property on January 25th, 1737. It requested that a road be laid out from the town of Lancaster to the Coventry Iron Works in Chester County and proper persons be appointed to lay out the road. The road was laid out December 6, 1737, and presented to the board that approved the draught and declared it was a Kings Highway or Public Road.[104]

## LABOR AT THE FRENCH CREEK IRON-WORKS

Partly as a result of their isolated locations, there were always labor shortages at the early Pennsylvania ironworks and ironmasters were always looking for ways to supplement their labor supply. Pennsylvania ironmasters used a combination of free laborers, redemptioners, indentured servants and African slaves. The Swedish historian, Rev. Israel Acrelius wrote in his discussion about the Chester County works: "Its discoverer is Mr. Nutt, who afterwards took Mr. Branz [Branson] into partnership. They both went to England, brought workmen back with them and continued together."

The later ironworks supplemented their labor force with what are called on the books, "day laborers." For the most part these were neighboring farmers who did the hauling, loading and even charcoal making or mining in their off seasons. However, because Nutt's ironworks were located so remotely, initially, no one lived nearby to hire.[105] Consequently, it would appear from reviewing *Coventry Forge Book B,* that early on, the majority of workers at the French Creek Iron-Works were white, indentured servants whose time was purchased at the Philadelphia wharf. Between 1727 and 1730, the works owned the time of at least 24 indentured servants who served as woodcutters, forgemen and colliers. Nine indentured servants completed their terms between 1727-1730.[106]

Indentured servants at this date generally served for a period of three years. Hermelin states that the cost for passage money of an able-bodied man was from £25 to £30 Pennsylvania currency. "For this amount such a servant must work for three years during which time he is given food and clothing, but no wages....Prior to the war [Revolutionary War] these servants were registered by a public clerk and their master was obliged to give a suit of clothing at the expiration of the period of service."[107]

Using indentured servants as a primary labor force had several disadvantages. First, after they served their time and claimed their freedom dues, they often left. This created the continual need for new workers and a constant retraining issue. Second, they continually ran away before their time was up. Also, during wartime, indentured servants were often able to reduce their bondage time by volunteering to enlist. Shortly after Samuel Nutt's death in 1740, Lieutenant Governor George Thomas issued a proclamation seeking volunteers to fight the Spanish. Ten indentured servants of Anna Nutt & Company answered his call. Nutt petitioned the Pennsylvania Assembly to recover what their departure had cost the business. Many of the enlistees were colliers who had "been instructed in their Business at considerable Expense." After they left, Nutt claimed production had to be halted causing several hundred pounds in damage to her and the other owners.[108]

In the 1720s, African slaves were just beginning to be used at the Pennsylvania ironworks. The estate accounting for the company at Nutt's (and his nephew's) death shows the company owned two Negroes worth £50 each. These two appear to be the "two able Negroes, good Work-men, one a Hammer-man the other a Finer" mentioned in the July 26, 1744, *Pennsylvania Gazette* when Anna Nutt tried to rent the forge. Nutt's personal estate accounting also lists two blacks: "A negro boy named Cudjo 30," and, "A negro boy named George 15."

In October 1726, Samuel Nutt was again elected to the Assembly as one of eight Freeman Representatives from Chester County.[109] During his 1726-1727 Assembly service, a proposal was made by "sundry Persons connected in the Iron-Works" that has been attributed to Nutt, who "unquestionably" introduced it. The petitioners specifically complained that "the Difficulty of getting Labourers, and their excessive Wages, [were] a great Discouragement and Hindrance to their Undertaking." They requested to be allowed to purchase slaves for their ironworks without paying Pennsylvania's duties on slaves. The question was eventually called and voted down. [110]

The fact that both indentured servants and African slaves at the ironworks often ran away, also created problems for the ironmaster. Advertisements placed in the newspapers though for their apprehension and return, create an exceptional resource for an ironwork researcher and often provide information not found elsewhere. Mittleberger in his 1750 Journal indicates that: "If such a runaway has been away from his master for a day, he must serve for it as a punishment one week, for a week a month, and for a month half a year."[111] Runaway indentured servants at the French Creek Works are mentioned several times in the various newspapers.

The October 13, 1726, *American Weekly Mercury* notes an indentured servant who served his time at French Creek in Pennsylvania, at the "Iron Works." The first Nutt advertisement was printed in the *American Weekly Mercury* March 19, 1730. Nutt indicates two servant men ran away from the "Iron-Works at French Creek in Chester County." Whoever shall take up said servants, should bring them to Samuel Nut at the Iron-Works at French Creek, or to William Branson in Philadelphia. A reward and reasonable charges were to be paid.

Samuel Nutt at the "French-Creek-Iron-Works Chester County Dec. 25, 1736," put an advertisement in the January 6, 1737, *American Weekly Mercury* concerning a runaway. He indicates: "Ran-way for Samuel Nutt, at the iron-works aforesaid, a Servant Man named David McQuatty, by Trade a Hammerman and Refiner..." Similar ads appeared in the January 13, July 7, and July 21 *Mercury*.

Additionally, after Nutt's death, Samuel Savage, at the "French Creek Iron Works, Chester County," put an advertisement for a runaway in the September 13, 1739, *Pennsylvania Gazette*; in a *Pennsylvania Gazette* article dated August 21, 1740, Henry Hockley, "near Nutt's Iron-

Works" noted a runaway, and William Gardiner and Adam Farquhar "of Nutt's Iron-Works, Chester County," put an advertisement in the *Pennsylvania Gazette* May 5, 1743, concerning a runaway.

## LAND ACQUISITIONS DURING FRENCH CREEK WORKS PERIOD

Iron refining needed large amounts of land for timber to be made into charcoal to be used as the fuel. As with most of the ironmasters during this time, the partners obtained land from the Penn government through warrant and patent. James Steel wrote a letter to surveyor John Taylor: "Our ffr^d Sam^1 Nutt having paid a Good sum of money to me for the Prop^rs use hath requested a further addition to his Lands to accommodate his Iron Works, which the Proprietary was pleased to Grant him."[112] Tracing Nutt and Branson's numerous purchases of large tracts of land during the 1720s and 1730s proves challenging and it is hard to track land they purchased. Depending on the tract, often large amounts of time were involved between the warrant date and the issue of the patent.

The amount of acreage also often differed between what was warranted and what was surveyed. From 1733 to 1752, Samuel Nutt warranted over 3,000 total acres and William Branson warranted 4,900 acres in Chester County.[113] The fact that both partners were warranting land in basically the same areas was apparently the cause of a dispute and strain on the partnership. Some of Branson's surveys were adjoining Nutt's land, and J. Steel, writing to John Taylor, November 26, 1735, says: "I have not seen Samuel Nutt since I received thy letter which informs me of his returns being sent up. I hope Wm. Branson's are also sent that thereby the long depending affair between them may be at length settled."[114]

Between December of 1733 and December of 1735, Samuel Nutt paid the Proprietaries £360 in five separate payments for various land he received or for surveys that were done. For the most part this land is noted as "near his Iron Works in Chester county."[115]

While often hard to decipher due to their brevity, the minutes of the Board of Property Meetings as found in the printed *Pennsylvania Archives* provide a good source of the two French Creek ironmasters' land acquisitions. The Minutes of the Property Meeting dated 6 1mo, 1733, indicate: "Sam'l Nutt requests the Grant of some lands adjoyning to his Iron works which the Prop'ry is pleased to Grant him and an Order is sent to John Taylor for the Purpose."[116]

Minutes of the Property Meeting dated 25th 12mo, 1734/35, indicate: "William Branson represents that the Land intended to be granted to Sam'l Nutt and himself falls much less in Quantity than what was design'd for them and therefore he desires that part of the land called Wynns for which they have little or no right may be added to the other for further Consideration."[117]

The Chester County Warrant Register pages show that in 1735, Samuel Nutt filed on four separate tracts in Coventry (one of which was patented by Thomas Potts in 1775). The warrant dated October 20, 1735, taking them up called for a total of 1,000 acres. The property was surveyed and the date of the return was February 16, 1735/36, and the actual acreage was over 1,100 acres.

Again, while hard to decifer, the Board of Property Minutes for 15th 4th mo 1736, record the purchase and others: "To Sam'l Nutt for two Tracts in Chester County, 300 Acres in Coventry, 600 Acres in Nantmell--959 by the Comm'rs Warr't in 1717 at £10 @ C't & 1s Sterl. quitr't. The Patent dated 8th 4mo 1736. To Sam'l Nutt for 4 Tracts in Chester County: 705 Acres in Nantmell, 277 Acres in Coventry, 64 Acres in Nantmell--1146. Granted by the Prop'rs Warr't in 1733 at £15:10 @ C't and a half peny Sterling @ Acre Quit rent. The Patent dated 8th 4mo'th 1736."[118]

## COVENTRY STEEL FURNACE BUILT

Sometime in the early 1730s, Samuel Nutt is credited with building a steel furnace on the French Creek at his works—the first in Pennsylvania. While its location is uncertain, it was probably near the other two ironworks. Its history is blanketed in obscurity and little documentation remains. Called in secondary sources the Coventry Steel Works and incorrectly, the Vincent Steel Works, they were probably built in conjunction with the company at their French Creek Iron-Works. William Branson also built steel works before 1750 in Philadelphia and is often credited with owning two. While it is certain the Philadelphia works were solely Branson's, the question remains if both partners or only Nutt built the one located at Coventry.

Bining indicates: "In 1732, Samuel Nutt, Sr., decided to experiment in the making of steel, and a steel furnace, the first in the Province, was built."[119] Unfortunately, he does not provide its location or how he came up with the date. Batchelder states simply: "At French Creek he [Nutt] made the first steel in America." This furnace had a short existence. It is not listed in Nutt's 1738 estate accounting, Samuel Nutt, Jr.'s 1739 estate accounting, or in Branson's 1741 lawsuit. The furnace is mentioned by Hermelin in 1783 when he was discussing the 1750 iron act: "Several blast furnaces and hammers, [the] Coventry steel furnace as well as three rolling and slitting works were already established..."[120]

While the Coventry furnace was closed by 1750, Branson had built a second in Philadelphia about 1747. This furnace gets confused with Nutt's furnace. Pennsylvania Proprietor Thomas Penn wrote William Branson's son-in-law Richard Hockley in 1750 after the passage of the Iron Act by Parliament, which stated:

> "No mill or other engine for slitting or rolling of iron, or any plating forge to work with a tilt hammer, or any furnace for the making of steel shall be erected" in the colonies: "I enclose you the Act: you will find there must not be any Steel Furnices or Slitting Mills erected. I think Mr. Branson has one of the first which you take care to keep upp and in time it may be of great advantage to you."[121]

Israel Acrelius' 1759 *History of New Sweden* states: "At French Creek, or Branz's Works, there is a steel furnace, built with a draught-hole, and called an 'air-oven.' In this, iron bars are set at the distance of an inch apart. Between them are scattered horn, coal dust, ashes, etc. The iron bars are thus covered with blisters, and this is called 'blister steel.' It serves as the best steel to put upon edge-tools…These steel-works are now said to be out of operation." Acrelius was in America from 1749 to 1756. John Owen, sheriff for Chester County, responding to the requirements of the 1750 Iron Act, indicated: "There is no plating-mill nor steel-furnace…in use [in Chester County] 24th June, 1750."[122]

The Coventry steelworks were still out of operation by 1764, when John Potts' son, Thomas Potts (1735-1785), obtained the property, consolidating the Potts and the Grace interests. Thomas and his brothers, Samuel and John, under the firm of Thomas Potts & Co., reopened them. To get around the restrictions imposed by the 1750 Iron Act, there are several Notes of Testimony, dated in 1764, found in *Letters of Attorney* from individuals indicating that the Steel Furnace Thomas Potts was repairing was the "same one belonging to Samuel Nutt."

In effect, even though they are now closed, they meet the requirements of the Act by having been open prior to 1750. John Taylor's closed Sarum Forge also became valuable as it had an existing slitting mill that was added in 1746. The documentation obtained shows there was a steel furnace in existence prior to 1750 at Coventry, but no dates are given. The new partners put an advertisement in the November 19, 1764, *Staatesbote* advertising their steel "cheaper than English steel" and gave purchasers the opportunity to try it before paying for it. Steel was produced there by Potts throughout the Revolution for the war effort. The closing date is unknown.

## IRONWORK GROWTH AND COVENTRYVILLE

Sometime in the early 1720s, Coventry Township was created, and it is assumed that it was named by Nutt. Nutt's Road was built in 1726, from the ironworks to the east and in 1738, a road was completed from the works to Lancaster to the west. These two roads became Ridge Road, later Route 23 which went right through the ironworks—the furnace was on the north side of the road and the forge on the south side. Each had their own dam and race. There are not any descriptions of the works at this time. In 1783, Dr. Johann David Schoepf who traveled west on Nutt's Road from Valley Forge, left the following: "The forge at Coventry stands in a narrow valley, running east and west."[123]

The initial "Dwelling House and a Forge with Engines belonging to their Iron Works besides other Building & Erections" grew into a larger complex. As the iron conglomeration expanded, the number of workers and animals needed to run it also grew. These workers needed lodging, food, goods, services and religious institutions; the animals needed forage, stables and fields. Food plots had to be established for both man and beast. The steel furnace was added about 1732. The laborers, who were initially mostly indentured servants, were eventually supplemented by free laborers who brought their families and they lived close by. A company store was initially built to supply some of their needs, but eventually other businesses and houses were established. This area eventually evolved into the village of Coventryville which grew up on Ridge Road to the east of the works.[124]

## SAMUEL NUTT JR. AND JOHN POTTS

It was during this time period, that Nutt's apparent nephew and namesake, Samuel Nutt, Jr. (c.1712-1739), came from England to work at the French Creek Works. The anecdotal story that gets repeated is Samuel Nutt was childless and he brought Samuel over to be his heir.[125] Their exact relationship has not been established. Batchelder calls Nutt "his namesake and heir." Samuel left the younger Nutt and his wife one-half of his estate by his 1737 will in which he calls him: "my Son in Law Samuel Nutt." The younger Nutt's exact date of arrival is unknown but he was in Chester County by the 1732/1733 tax return on which he is listed as a freeman and taxed £0-7-6. On May 17, 1733, "Samuel Nutt" and Rebecca Savage, youngest daughter of Anna Savage Nutt, married at Christ Church in Philadelphia.[126] It is generally considered to have been an arranged marriage that the younger people found satisfactory. One child, given as "Anna Nutt, Jr.," was born of the union in 1736-37. This child would marry Thomas Potts, the eldest son of John Potts and later ironmaster at Coventry Forge. Samuel and Rebecca would both play a part in the establishment of Warwick Furnace.

On April 11, 1734, a second marriage took place that would also have implications for the French Creek Iron-Works. John Potts (1710-1768) "of Colebrook Dale, Founder," twenty-four-year-old son of Colebrook Dale Furnace ironmaster Thomas Potts, married Ruth Savage, Rebecca's sister, of the Township of Coventry. Though the marriage certificate was Quaker-like, they were married by Joseph Brinton, Justice of the Peace. The certificate as presented in the *Potts Memorial* indicates that the couple was married at Nutt's home: "Now these are to certify all whom it may concern, that in order to accomplish these said intentions of marriage they, the said parties, being at the house of Samuel Nutt, in the township of Coventry, and county of Chester...."

Along with numerous Potts and Savage relatives, "Sam[ll] Nutt" and Anna Nutt signed the marriage certificate along with "Samuel Nutt, Jr." and Rebecca Nutt.[127]   Due to a number of early deaths, Potts would eventually take control of the Nutt iron interests.

On March 25, 1734, Samuel Nutt and Richard Jones were appointed guardians of the nine children of Evan Evans of Uwchlan Township.[128] Samuel Nutt was also named the executor of the 1736 will of John Rutter, the son of Thomas Rutter and his wife's brother. John Rutter and Nutt had both invested in the 1726 Abington Furnace in Delaware. As executors, Nutt and Rutter's wife, Mary, put the standard request for accounting in the February 10th and 17th *American Weekly Mercurys*. Samuel and Mary put another notice in the September 22nd *Pennsylvania Gazette* concerning the estate: "House and lot in Market St., Phila,. lately in possession of John Rutter, dec'd, and 138 acres of land between Colebrookdale Furnace and Pine Forge - will be sold by Mary Rutter and Samuel Nutt, executors."

## SAMUEL SAVAGE

About this time, Anna's son Samuel Savage (c.1706-1742) began to be involved in the ironworks. He would play an important, though brief role in both the French Creek Iron-Works and the new Warwick

Furnace. Samuel was born around 1706 in Philadelphia County. His father died when he was about age 12 and his mother married Samuel Nutt when he was an older teenager. The family moved to Coventry at the time of the marriage and he learned the iron trade from his grandfather, Thomas Rutter, or his step-father, Samuel Nutt.

In 1728, Savage was one of the witnesses of the will of Isaac Taylor of Thornbury, Chester County. In 1729, Savage first appears on the Coventry tax roles as a "freeman" and appears again in 1730. In 1733, Savage is listed on the tax roles not as a freeman but as a property holder. At this time he married Ann(e) Taylor, daughter of Isaac and Martha (Roman) Taylor. Ann's grandfather, John Taylor, had come to Pennsylvania from Wiltshire, England, in 1684, and became surveyor General of Chester County. He was the surveyor of all of Samuel Nutt's early warrant tracts. John's son, Isaac Taylor, Ann's father, served as Chester's Deputy Surveyor General. Much of the early information presented by Furthey and Cope about Nutt came from the Taylor papers.

Ann's family belonged to the Society of Friends and Concord Meeting records for 7mo 3, 1733, note: "Ann Savage formerly Taylor having been educated amongst Friends contrary to known rules She went and was married by a priest where for the Meeting appoints Ann Downing and _____ Miller to reproach her." On 8mo 8, the Women's meeting noted that there was testimony against her which was left for publication by the Men's meeting. On 12mo 4, 1733, she was disowned by the Concord Monthly Meeting for her marriage by a priest to Savage.[129] Ann's brother, John Taylor, built Sarum Forge in 1739 on Chester Creek to use Warwick's iron in the 1740s when Samuel Savage was running it.

The following year, 1734, Samuel Savage was taxed £16. On 16 February 1735, Samuel and his brother Thomas each filed for a warrant for 100-acre tracts of land in Chester County.[130] When his heirs sold his property after his death, the deed notes: "and 150 acres, in Coventry, granted by Warrant to Samuel Savage, February 16, 1735…and 85 acres in Coventry, Warrant, February 16, 1735, surveyed to Samuel Savage in right of Thomas Savage and 148 acres, surveyed by warrant, February 16, 1735, to Samuel Savage."[131]  Additionally, on 12 August 1736, Samuel Nutt and wife Anna of Coventry, by deed sold to Samuel Savage of the same township, blacksmith, son of said Anna, 215 acres in Coventry, which was part of 300 acres bought of James Pugh.[132]

George Taylor arrived at Coventry at this time. Taylor, who would later marry Savage's widow, was born in Ireland and immigrated to Philadelphia in 1736, as an indentured servant. His indenture was purchased by Samuel Savage. Taylor started as a laborer at the French Creek Iron-Works, but eventually was made the bookkeeper.[133] He in time became an ironmaster and after marrying Savage's widow was involved in running both Coventry and Warwick. He later rented Durham Furnace and was a signer of the Declaration of Independence.

Based on taxes, it appears that by 1735, Samuel had built a house on the 100-acre tract he warranted for himself. The property was located on the French Creek in Chester County near Coventry and he lived there. He is shown on the tax roles in Coventry as a property holder for 1735, 1735/6, 1737, and 1737/38. His tax for each year was £20. Additionally, on 9 September 1736, Samuel Savage, yeoman of Coventry Township, mortgaged the 215-acre tract he had obtained from Samuel Nutt to the Loan Office for £45.00, the payment of which was due 23 January 1758.[134]

By 1736, things looked good for the French Creek Iron-Works. Samuel Nutt was in his prime and three young men, Samuel Nutt, Jr., Samuel Savage and John Potts were all seasoned ironworkers. A new furnace on Rock Run would replace the older one that year and Nutt was probably already considering building another furnace separate from Branson. The future looked bright. But in five years, three of the four above mentioned ironmasters would be dead and the Works at Coventry would go through a number of transitions and management changes.

# ROCK RUN FURNACE
# AT COVENTRY REPLACED,
# 1736

*"...and ascribing this Decay of Trade to the Erection of Iron-works in his Majesty's Plantations in America, whereby those Colonies have been induced to set up the Iron Manufacture, and furnish themselves with such Iron Wares, as must otherwise been supplied with from Great Britain, as they were before such Iron-works were erected."*

A PETITION OF THE IRONMONGERS AND
MANUFACTURERS OF IRON,
*NEW YORK GAZETTE*, JUNE 19, 1738

In 1736, Samuel Nutt was 61 years old; William Branson was 54 years old. They had been partners for 16 years. Their business dealings had been financially advantageous, and as a result, both were properous men. It would appear that about 1736, two furnaces, both named Reading, were built. One was built (or rebuilt) by Samuel Nutt and William Branson to replace the older 1725 one on Rock Run in Nantmeal Township; and one was built outside the company on the south branch in Nantmeal. But, as with all the ironworks on French Creek, there is some confusion surrounding when they were built and initally who owned them. Isabella Batchelder in the *Potts Memorial*, quotes an unnamed document providing the only information on the new furnace:

"The 15th day of March, 1736, Samuel Nutt and William Bronson entered into an agreement with John Potts to carry on their furnace called **Redding, recently built near Coventry**, and of which they are styled "**joint owners**." He was "to cast the quantity of twenty-eight hundred weight of Cart-Boxes, Sash Weights or any other Particular small Castings every Month during the Continuance of the said Blast And they also covenant that they y' said Owners or their Clerks or Agents for the Time being, shall deliver no Quantity of Rum to any of the People Belonging to the Furnace or therein concerned, without a Note or Token from the said John Potts or his Agents or Assistants."[135]

Consequently, Batchelder assumed that the furnace they had recently built was the Reading Furnace associated with William Branson. (This is definitely a different furnace than Branson's, as his was still "errecting" in January of 1737.) As a result, she states that Nutt owned half of (Branson's) Reading Furnace. However, the furnace that John Potts was to carry on was the one that is listed in Nutt's estate accounting as the "old furnace." Branson and Nutt each owned one-half of this furnace. The individuals taking Nutt's estate inventory in May of 1738 noted: "A Ring [that was owned by both Branson and Nutt] Round the shaft of the **old Furnace**" and "one ton of sow mettle [that Nutt owned] at the **new furnace** [Warwick]."

Based on the information available, it would appear that the original 1725 furnace on Rock Run was replaced by a newer one by Nutt and Branson on Nutt-owned land in 1736. This new furnace was initially called "Redding," but later changed to Rock Run.[136] John Potts was hired as the ironmaster. It apparently was built on the site of the original furnace and used the same race. While it seems odd, William Branson built another furnace on his land in Nantmeal (now East Nantmeal) in 1736 and also called it Reading.

Rock Run Furnace should not be confused with the "650 acres land in Nantmeal on which the new furnace is building, with sundry out houses" mentioned in Nutt's estate. This furnace is Warwick, which by that time was already being constructed. Nutt's 1736 will shows he and Branson both owned one half of the Rock Run Furnace:

"One half of all my Right to the Furnace and Forgge, together with all Buildings thereunto belonging; secondly, the halfe of all my Right to the Lands whereon they stand or are Appropriate there- unto, viz: The halfe my shear of a hundred acres whereon the fforggo standeth and the halfe of the Land whereon the Furnace standeth, and to her heirs forever."

Although unsure, it would appear that Rock Run was closed by 1741, when Branson filed his countersuit against Anna Nutt. He indicates that he owned a moiety of an ironwork called a forge but no furnace is mentioned. The name of the furnace had been changed by 1743, to Rock Run Furnace when it was apparently continued or reopened by John Potts. The book by that name at the Pennsylvania Archives shows that Potts ran the furnace from 1743 until 1747. Rock Run supplied most of the Potts' family's forges and also William Bird's forges. Rock

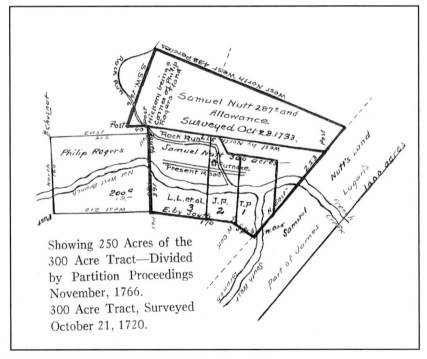

Showing 250 Acres of the 300 Acre Tract—Divided by Partition Proceedings November, 1766.
300 Acre Tract, Surveyed October 21, 1720.

*Rock Run Furnace Location*[137]

Run Furnace appears to have closed after that time, as Potts began spending time at the newer Warwick Furnace. He made Warwick into one of the Province's largest and most important furnaces. A gristmill was built beside the Rock Run Furnace after it closed to use the old race and replaced it completely. Furthey and Cope state in 1904 on their write-up on Charles James: "In 1859 Mr. James engaged in the milling business on Rock Run creek, and in 1872 removed...[to] the old Reading Furnace controlled by Nutt & Branson." The mill and its ruins were in existence for many years.

*Ten Plate Stove cast at Warwick Furnace in the nineteenth century currently exhibited at Hopewell Furnace National Historic Site in Tenant House Two.*

# PART III

## FRENCH CREEK IRON-WORKS
## AFTER SAMUEL NUTT, 1738

*Ten Plate Stove cast at Warwick Furnace in the nineteenth century on exhibit in the Boarding House at Hopewell Furnace National Historic Site.*

# DEATH AND ESTATE DISTRIBUTION, 1738

*"And this Deponant doth further say that William Branson never had any part in Warwick Furnace, nor had the said Samuel Nutt any part in Reading Furnace."*

RACHAEL JONES, 1806

Samuel Nutt became ill in 1737 and died about 1738. His exact date of death is unknown, but is assumed to be in late 1737 or early 1738. He wrote his will, which was dated September 25, 1737. (See Appendix 1.) Basically, Nutt left half his estate to his wife and the other half to Samuel Nutt, Jr. He had died prior to February 1739. Thomas Savage received a patent for 210 acres on land originally warranted in 1719 by Nicholas Rogers on one of the branches of French Creek. The patent, recorded February ye 23d 1738/39 [1739], indicated it touched William Branson's property and the "Land late of Samuel Nutt deceased."

On March 9th, 1737/38, Joseph Phippes, Nathan Phippes and John Phippes took Samuel Nutt's Last Will and Testament to Chester for probate. It was recorded in *Chester County Will Book D, Vol. 4,* Page 2 and numbered 626. His estate was inventoried by William Boone, and brothers-in-law Edward Rees and Henry Hockley on the 25th and 26th of May, 1738. The estate was broken down into two parts: his personal estate and the estate he owned with Branson in the company.[138]

This extensive inventory of Samuel Nutt's estate is found at the Chester County Archives. The inventory of his estate indicates that the items he owned with William Branson amounting to the sum of £2912, which was to be divided equally between them. His private estate amounted to £5444, which was an extremely large sum for that day. Some of the items from his inventory are shown here:

From inventory of company estate:

| | |
|---|---|
| A Ring Round the shaft at the old Furnace and an old Broken hammer 10 cwt | 1.5.0 |
| 100 Load of coal at the ffurnace | 100.0.0 |
| 24 tonn pigg iron | 130.0.0 |
| 10 husks, weight one tonn | 5.1.0 |
| 730 loads of coal at the fforge | 730.0.0 |
| 2 Negroes at £50 each | 100.0.0 |
| 250 acres of land with the fforge, dwelling and sundry out houses erected thereon | 1500.0.0 |

From inventory of private estate:

| | |
|---|---|
| One ton of sow mettle at new furnace | 5.10.0 |
| 18 stove plates, 10 cwt | 8.16.0 |
| The mine tract containeing 250 acres of land. | 1500.0.0 |
| 650 acres land in Nantmill on which the new furrnace is building, with sundry out houses | 525.0.0 |
| 287 acres land in Coventry being the land on which Samuel Nutts house stands | 300.0.0 |
| A negro boy named Cudjo | 30.0.0 |
| A negro boy named George | 15.0.0 |
| 2 hhds Rum | 26.1.3 |
| 78 ells of Ozenbrigs | 7.7.0 |

## COVENTRY WORKS, POST SAMUEL NUTT

Samuel Nutt's death did not dissolve the company that ran the French Creek Iron-Works, but relationships between William Branson and Nutt's heirs did not improve after his death. The furnace which would become Rock Run Furnace and the Coventry Refinery Forge were still half owned by both Branson and Nutt's heirs. Nutt had left half his estate to his wife, and half to his nephew, Samuel Nutt, Jr. He stipulated in his will that another furnace should be built, it was named Warwick and in blast perhaps in 1738. It was initially managed by the younger Nutt and his brother-in-law, Samuel Savage. The Rev. Israel Acrelius noted the Nutt/Branson break-up: "Each has his own furnace – Branz at Reading, Nutt in Warwick. Each also has his own forges – Branz in Windsor, Nutt supplies four forges besides his own in Chester County."[139]

The nine-year period between Nutt's death and the closing of Rock Run Furnace is a complicated one to document and the exact ending of the French Creek Iron-Works is unknown. Basically, the French Creek Company run by Nutt was gradually replaced by the Warwick Company which was eventually run by John Potts. However, the two ran simultaneously for a few years. The death of Samuel Nutt, followed soon after by the deaths of Samuel Nutt, Jr., and Samuel Savage, and the quick remarriages of their widows to Robert Grace and George Taylor caused a confusing array of short-lived new companies to be formed, and involved a new set of ironmasters running the ironworks. By 1743, Branson was running Reading Furnace and was not involved with Warwick or Coventry. John Potts, under the firm of Grace and Potts was running Warwick Furnace, Rock Run Furnace was closed, and Coventry Forge, while not part of the Warwick Company, was refining Warwick iron and eventually owned by John Potts' son, Thomas.

## COVENTRY AND ROCK RUN FURNACE

As stipulated by Nutt's will, in 1738-1739, the younger Nutt and Anna's son, Samuel, built and ran the new Warwick Furnace while they continued to run the old French Creek Iron-Works. In 1739, probably in the late winter or early spring, two deaths occurred simultaneously that affected this arrangement. Anna's son, Thomas Savage and Samuel Nutt Jr. died about the same time; Savage had a will, Nutt died intestate. Thomas Savage's will was written February 24, 1739. He left most of his estate to his brother, Samuel. Both deceased men's estates were taken to Chester County Courthouse and filed on 6th of June 1739. On the same date, Anna Nutt, Samuel Savage, and Henry Hockley provided Sureties for an Administrative Bond for Samuel Nutt, dec., Rebecca Nutt, administrator.

On February 12-14, 1739, Henry Hockley and William Branson did an inventory of the younger Samuel Nutt's estate. As with Samuel Nutt, Sr.'s estate, the inventory was broken down by Nutt's personal estate (some of which he owned with the widow Nutt) and what he owned with William Branson.[140] His estate was valued at over £8,000 including his share of Warwick Furnace, which was valued at £2,000.

At the younger Nutt's death, Warwick and the French Creek Iron-Works were now owned half by Anna (Savage) Nutt, and half by Rebecca Nutt, the younger Nutt's widow. When Samuel Savage put a notice in the September 13, 1739, *Pennsylvania Gazette* concerning a runaway, he was apparently the manager of the works for his mother and sister.

About a year after her husband's death, on May 23, 1740, the widow Rebecca (Savage) Nutt married Robert Grace, a friend of Benjamin Franklin. The *American Weekly Mercury* and the *Pennsylvania Gazette* dated Sunday, May 29, 1740, had the following: "We hear from French-Creek in Chester County, that on Monday last Mr. Robert Grace, a Gentleman of this City, was married to Mrs. Rebecca Nutt, an agreeable young Gentle-woman, with a considerable Fortune." Grace, who had studied metalurgy in Europe, fairly quickly became involved in running the company, initially at the forge.[141]

## SAMUEL SAVAGE, ROBERT GRACE AND ANNA NUTT & CO.

Between Samuel Nutt, Jr.'s death in 1739, and his own in 1742, Samuel Savage was the senior ironmaster of his family's Coventry/Warwick interests. Savage was named executor for the February 24, 1739, will of his brother Thomas. He was left Thomas' "plantation and tract of Land in Nantmel township" and much of the estate. This property was between

Coventry and Warwick.[142] The deaths of both the younger Samuel Nutt and Thomas Savage had a major impact on management at Coventry and Warwick. At their deaths, Samuel Savage took over running Warwick Furnace, which was owned jointly by his mother and widowed sister. Robert Grace began managing Coventry Forge for the family. Abraham Hingle, a teamster, noted the following in September: "Received Sepr the 10, 1739, from Anna & Rebecca Nutt thirty-three Pigs weight one Tun which I Promise to Deliver unto White & Taylor, merchants in Philadelphia… Sept 29, 1739, Received of Anna and Rebecca Nutt Pigg & Pieces which I Promise to Deliver to John Reynolds in Philadelphia."[143]

Additionally, from November 6th to November 22nd, 1739, Anna Nutt, also given as the Widow Nutt, sent twelve loads of pig iron to the Pennsylvania's Proprietor, Thomas Penn. It was noted that "these Prizes were agreed for 7.10 - p Ton wth Bird Hockley."[144]

As a result of the younger Nutt's death and the fact that Samuel began managing the furnace, in 1740, Anna Nutt, Samuel's mother re-adjusted her ownership share and gave Samuel a 1/5th ownership. A similar agreement was reached on ore ownership.[145] At this time, Anna owned 3/10's, Samuel owned 2/10's and his sister, and widow of Samuel Nutt, Jr.,

*Coventry House—Robert and Rebecca (Savage) Grace's Home*[146]

owned a 5/10th share. Warwick Furnace was run as "Samuel Savage & Co." until Samuel's death in 1742. During his management, Savage's brother-in-law, John Taylor, opened Sarum Forge to use Warwick's iron. Savage signed as one of the witnesses of the will of Samuel Washburn of Nantmel Township dated 30 August 1741. Washburn was a clerk at Warwick.

Robert Grace's entry into the management of the Nutt interests seemed to have exacerbated the already strained relationship between Nutt's partner at Coventry, William Branson and the Nutt/Savage family. In Chester County, at the August Quarter Sessions Court, 1741, suit was brought against William Branson in the name of Anna Nutt, Robert Grace and Samuel Savage. Branson was charged with taking iron ore from their property. At the same term, Branson brought suit against Anna Nutt, Robert Grace, Gent., and Rebecca his wife.[147] Branson's suit is interesting as it lists his holdings and provides a good contemporary description of Coventry in 1741: "the moiety of Five messuages, Two Hundred and Fifty acres of Land and the moiety of one Iron Work called a Forge, Three Coal-Houses with the appurtenances, all situate in Coventry...and also of the moiety of an Iron mine with six acres of Land."[148]

Shortly after the lawsuit was filed, on September 22, 1741, Samuel Savage, apparently ill, wrote his will. He died testate in early spring of 1742. His will was filed in *Chester County Will Bk. 2*, p. 107. William Jones, Robert Hogg, and James Speary were witnesses. It was taken for probate by Speary May 26, 1742. (See Appendix 3 for the complete will.) The inventory of Samuel Savage was taken by Aubrey Roberts and Sam'l Flower and filed November 26, 1744. (Chester County No. 791.) His personal estate was estimated at £124.15.1. His inventory included five cows, two horses, Sundry Smiths tools, a servant lad, and a Negro woman.

## JOHN POTTS AND GEORGE TAYLOR

On December 17, 1741, less than three months after Samuel Savage wrote his will, John Potts of Philadelphia leased one-half of Warwick Furnace from Robert Grace. This would have been Rebecca Nutt

Grace's share. The Articles of Agreement were witnessed by Anna Nutt and George Taylor.[149] After this time, Potts began to be actively involved in managing Warwick. At the same time, he took over the Rock Run Furnace operation at Coventry and for about six years, both furnaces were active. After Savage's death, Potts would form a company with his brother-in-law, Robert Grace and move to Warwick Furnace where he would remain. By 1743, "Mrs. Nutt and Robert Grace" were dealing in iron. Rock Run Furnace was eventually closed and merged with Warwick.

George Taylor, who was working at Warwick, married Anne (Taylor) Savage and worked at both Coventry and Warwick. Samuel Savage's portion of Warwick and the ore mines was left to his son, who inherited it at age 21 (1754). Taylor remained for several years but left and moved to Durham Furnace, which he initially ran in connection with Samuel Flower. By that time, John Potts was managing the furnace. Potts would be credited for building Warwick into one of Pennsylvania's largest and his sons, grandsons and great-grandsons managed it until the mid-1800s. Potts carried on Samuel Nutt's legacy.

*Oil painting, "Hopewell Furance," by Antony Lamor, dated 1854. Oil painting on canvas depicting an iron furnace believed to be Hopewell. The furnace is in blast, and the painting is dominated by the huge column of smoke pouring from the stack. The painting is the only known illustration of the furnace community in production.* Picture courtesy of Hopewell Furnace.

# APPENDICES

**WILLS AND BRIEF HISTORIES
OF READING,
WARWICK AND COVENTRY**

# APPENDIX 1

## WILL OF SAMUEL NUTT (c.1680-1738), CHESTER COUNTY WILL BOOK D-2

In the name of God Amen. I Samuel Nutt of Coventry in the County of Chester and Province of Pennsylvania being in a disposing Mind and Memory Praised be God, therefor, and calling to Mind the uncertainty of this Mortal Life and it is Appointed for all men once to die, Do make and ordaine this my Last Will and Testament, Revoaking and Disanuling all former Wills by me made.

Item. I Give and Bequeath unto my Dear & Loving Wife Anna Nutt after all my Debts and Furnerall Charges paid, One halfe of all my Right to the Furnace and Forgge togeather with all Buildings thereunto belonging, secondly the halfe of all my Right to the Lands whereon they Stand or are Appropriate thereunto. Viz: The halfe my Shear of a Hundred Acres whereon the fforge standeth and the halfe of the Land Or Tract whereon the Furnace standeth and to her Heirs for Ever.

Item. I likewise Give unto her all my Land that Leyeth on the Northern Side of a Line Run West and by North from the South West Corner of Henry Hockley's Field on the North Side of the Mine Road to another Line drawn from the Line Run on the East side of Thomas Savage's Field and where it Crosses a Runn on the same Side a little above his house, and from thence to the South East corner of the Mine Tract, and to her Heirs ffor Ever.

Item. I likewise give unto her One hundred & twenty acres of Land on the North side of the South Branch of the French Creek in Such a place as she shall think proper to Build a Furnace on, Provided it be not above one hundred and thirty Perches in Length upon the said Creek and to her Heirs, with Liberty to Cut as much Timber of the adjacent Land as Build the same.

Item. I likewise Give unto her and her Heirs ffor Ever that house that Samuel Nutt Jun: bought at Lancaster with the Lott where on it is Built, and a Five Acre Lott also some distance from the said House.

Item. I likewise Give unto her one halfe of all my Bonds Bills and Book Debts & ca.

Item. I likewise Give unto her halfe my Stock of Pigg Iron, Barr Iron, Coals and hardewood & Ca .

Item. I likewise Give unto her halfe my Parssonall Estate of what Sort kind or Quallity soever.

Item. I likewise Give unto her halfe my Emproved or Clear'd Land.

Item. I likewise Give and Bequeath unto her One hundred and Fifty Acres of Land that lyeth next to Phillip Rogers, in the form of an Oblong and to her Heirs ffor Ever.

Item. I give and bequeath to my Son in Law Samuel Savage all my Wearing Apparrell of any kind whatever.

Item. I Give and Bequeath unto my well beloved Friend John Blaufoy of Eversham in Worcester Sheer in Great Brittain One hundred and fifty Pounds Current Money of Pensilvania, to be paid one halfe in on & Year after my Deceased and the other halfe in two years in full of all Acc'ts betwixt us.

Item. I give and Bequeath unto the Heirs of Thomas Crook of Hay Park in York Shire Great Brittaine Fifty Pounds Current Money of Pensilvania to be paid in two payments as above to be Left in the Care of William Hudson of Philadelphia.

Item. All the rest of my Estate both Real and Parsonall I Give and Bequeath unto my Son in Law Samuel Nutt and Rebeca his Wife and to their Heirs ffor Ever.

And I do hereby Constitute and Appoint my trusty and well beloved Friends Jonathan Robeson Esqr and _____ to assist my Execrs to perform this my Last Will and Testament, and desire that Each of them would accept of halfe a Tonn Barr Iron, which I hereby. Give them. Lastly I do hereby Constitute and Appoint my well beloved

Wife Anna Nutt and my Son in Law Samuel Nutt to be my Executors to this my Last Will and Testament Signed Seal'd and Declear'd and Published to be my last Will and Testament the Twenty fifth day of September in the Eleventh Year of the Reign of our Sovereign Lord George the Second, One Thousand Seven Hundred and Thirty Seven.

SAMLL NUTT. [SEAL.]

In the Presence of us
NB the Erazement in the twenty first
Line being made before the Signing
and Sealing hereof.
Jo. PHIPPS  NATHAN PHIPPS  JOHN PHIPPS.

# APPENDIX 2

## WILL OF ANNA (RUTTER) SAVAGE NUTT
## (1686-1760),
### *PHILADELPHIA COUNTY WILL BOOK L-497*

In the Name of God the twenty Second Day of May in the Year of our
Lord One thousand seven Hundred and forty four I Anna Nutt
Widow and Relict to Samuel Nutt late of Coventry in the County
of Chester in the Province of Pennsylvania Iron Master deceased being weak in Body but of perfect Mind and Memory thanks be given
unto God therefore calling unto Mind the Mortality of my Body
and knowing it's appointed for all once to dye do make and ordain
this my last Will and Testament in manner following

Imprimis it is my Will that all my Debts and funeral Charges be first
paid.

Item, I give & Bequeath unto my Daughter Rebecca Grace Fifty Pounds
to be paid in five years after my Decease if she so long live but incase
of her Death before that time the same is to be paid to her daughter
Anna Nutt when she shall arrive at the age of Eighteeen Years but in
case she shou'd dye before that time without Issue then the same to
be paid to her Mother Rebecca Grace if living if not the same equally
divided amongst the Children of my said Sons Samuel and Joseph
dec.d or such of them as shall be then living

Item, I give and Bequeath unto my said Grand Daughter Anna Nutt on
half part of my plate

Item, I give and Bequeath unto my Grand Son Samuel Savage twenty
Pounds to be paid him when he shall arrive at the age of Eighteen
Years but in case of his Death before that time without Issue then the

same to be equally divided amongst the Children of Joseph Savage dec.ed or such of them as shall be then living

Item, I give and Bequeath unto my Grand Daughter Ann Savage Twenty Pounds to be paid to her at the age of Sixteen Years if she so long live but if she dyes before that time without Issue the same to be equally divided amongst her Brother and three Sisters or such of them as shall be then living and in case of all their Deaths without Issue to be equally divided amongst the Children of Joseph Savage or such of them as shall be then living

Item, It's my will and I hereby order that my Grand Children Samuel and Rebecca Savage Children of Joseph Savage decd be brought up by my Execur. hereafter named and have a Tolerable Education out of my Estate the former till he is fourteen years of age the latter thil she is sixteen, and further I give and Bequeath unto each of them fifty pounds to be paid in manner following vizt To Samuel Savage when he shall arrive at the age of twenty one Years and to Rebecca when she shall arrive at the age of Eighteen but if either of them dye before the time of payment without Issue then the Right of him or her so dying to be paid the survivor and in case of both their Deaths without Issue before the time of payment then the same to be equally divided amongst the Children of Samuel Savage decd or such of them as shall then be living

Item, I give and bequeath unto my Sister Hester Hockley the sum of Tenn pounds

Item, I give and Bequeath unto Thomas Rutter son of Joseph Rutter decd the sum of Tenn pounds to be paid him at the age of twenty one years if he so long live but if he dyes before he arrives at the age of Twenty one years then the same to be paid to Thomas Rutter son of John Rutter at the age of twenty one years

Item, I give and Bequeath unto Anna Hockley five pounds

Item, I give and Bequeath to the Overseers of Philada Baptist Meeting for the use of said Meeting the sum of Tenn Pounds.

Item, I give and Bequeath unto my son in Law John Potts all my Book Debts Bills Bonds Mortgages and all other my Personal Estate and Effects whatsoever which by this Will is not before bequeathed

And Lastly I give bequeath and Devise unto my said Son in Law John Potts whom I hereby Constitute make and Ordain Sole Executor of this my last Will and Testament all and Singular my Land Messuages & Tenements Together with my part of Warwick Furnace my part of the forges and Iron Mine and all other my real Estate whatsoever and wheresoever to Hold unto him the said John Potts his Heirs & assigns forever And I do hereby disallow revoke and disanull all and every former Testament Wills Legacies and Executors by me in any way before this time named willed and Bequeathed ratifying and confirming this and no other to be my Last Will & Testament

In Witness whereof I have hereunto set my Hand & Seal the day & year first above written Anna Nutt (seal)

Signed Sealed Published pronounce and Declared by the said Anna Nutt as her last Will and Testament in the presence of Marcus Hullings Wm Bird   Thos Yorke

# APPENDIX 3

## WILL OF SAMUEL SAVAGE (c.1706-1742),
## *CHESTER COUNTY WILL BOOK B-107*

Be it Remembered That I Samuel Savage of the Township of East Nantmel in the County of Chester in the Province of Pennsilvania Lying
at present under an Indisposition of Body but of Sound Memory
and Judgment do make this my Last Will and Testament Revoking
and Annulling all Others done heretofore.

My Will is that all my Just and Lawful Debts and Funeral Charges be
in the first place Satisfied and paid out of my Personal Estate By my
Beloved Spouse Ann Savage who I hereby Nominate and Appoint
to be my Executor

My Will is And I Give and Bequeath Unto the said Ann Savage my
Spouse Her Liferent use of the Rents Issues and Profits of my Two
Plantations Viz: One whereof Lying in the said Township of East
Nantmel and County aforesaid and the other Lying in Coventry
Township and County Aforesaid to be possessed and Enjoyed dur-
ing all the days of her Lifetime Under such Situation as is hereafter
mentioned. That it is

My Will that they shall not Clear the Land of Improving of the said
Plantations And that there shall not be Exceeded fifty Acres on Each
Plantation Besides who is All ready Cleared

My Will is And I Give and Bequeath Unto Ann Savage my said Spouse
the Rents Issues and Profits of my share and part of the Iron Furnace
Called Warwick (all Necessary and Incident Charges being deduct-
ed) To be possessed and Enjoyed by her until my Son Samuel Savage
Arrived to the Age of Twenty One Years In Consideration whereof

I Appoint and Ordain the said Ann Savage my Beloved Spouse to
Maintain Educate & Bring up my Children Samuel, Anna, Martha,
Ruth and Mary  Conform to their Rank and Station

My Will is And I Give and Bequeath Unto the said Samuel Savage my
Son so Soon as he Arrives to the Age of Twenty one Years All my part
and share of said Furnace Called Warwick To have and hold the said
part and share of said Furnace with all and Sundry the Appurtances
Unto him the said Samuel Savage my son his heirs and Assigns for
Ever

My Will is And I Give and Bequeath my said two Plantations Lying in
the Townships of Nantmel and Coventry aforesaid as and after the
decease of the said Ann Savage my Spouse Unto the said Samuel
Savage and to my Daughers Anna, Martha, Ruth and Mary, Equally
and proportionally to be divided betwixt them Share and Share alike
To have and to hold the said Two Plantations with the Appurtances
Unto them my said Children Samuel, Anna, Martha Ruth and Mary
in manner as Aforesaid Their heirs and Assigns For Ever

My Will is That is my said Son Samuel Savage Shall see Cause to pay the
sum of Two Hundred and fifty pounds Current money of Pennsilvania (After the decease of my said Spouse and Executrix Ann Savage)
Unto my four Daughters, Anna, Martha, Ruth and Mary  That is
to say To Each of them a like Share of the said Two hundred and
fifty pounds aforesaid or to their heirs or Assigns.  That then I Give
and Bequeath all that my Plantation which was my Brother Thomas
Savage Lying in Nantmel Township and County aforesaid to my said
Son Samuel Savage and his heirs and Assigns for Ever

My Will And  I give and Bequeath unto my Daughter Ann Savage the
sum of fifty Pounds to be paid to her at her arrival at the age of Eighteen Years, And to my Daughter Martha the sum of fifty Pounds to
be paid to her when She Arrives at the age of eighteen years.  And
to my Daughter Ruth the sum of fifty Pounds to be paid to her
when She Arrives to the age of Eighteen Years.  And Likewise to my
Daughter Mary the sum of fifty Pounds when She Arrives to the Age
of Eighteen Years, The which sums in all Extending to Two Hundred
Pounds, I Ordain to be paid In Current money of Pennsylvania By

my Executrix Unto my said children their Heirs and Assigns for Ever Respectively, But in Case any of my Children shall dye before they arrive to the age of Eighteen Years and Leave not Issue then her or their Portions To Return and be Equally divided amoungst my Surviving Children. All to be raised out of my Personal Estate and paid to them by my Sd Spouse and Executrix their Mother

My Will is And for the Better Enabling my Beloved Spouse Ann Savage to bring up and Educate my said five Children that is to Say, Samuel, Anna, Martha, Ruth, and Mary, without any Charge or Diminution of their sd Portions. I Give and Bequeath Unto the sd Ann Savage my Beloved Spouse all the Residue and Remainder of my Personal Estate (after paying the Debts and Legacies mentioned) To be Disposed of by her at her Pleasure

And Lastly I Nominate and Appoint John Taylor, Henry Hockley, and John Potts to assist the said Ann Savage my Beloved spouse to put this my will into Execution and I Appoint my Executrix to pay Each of them the sum of Tenn Pounds Lawful money of Pennsilvania of my Personal Estate in twelve months after my Decease for their Trouble and pain they shall be at on this Account, And I do hereby Authorize And Impower the sd John Taylor, Henry Hockley, and John Potts, that in Case my sd Spouse Ann Savage my Executrix should alter her Condition by Marrying again That in such Case the sd John Taylor, Henry Hockley, and John Potts if they see Cause shall Demand Security for the payment of the sd four Childrens Portions This is to Say Ann, Martha, Ruth, and Mary Savage. But upon Refusal of such Security it is my will the sd Childrens Portions Together with the Charges arising by such Sale And the money to be put into good and Able Bond, Until the Children aforesaid Come to Age And then to be paid To Each of them as they shall Arrive at the Age of Eighteen Years.

In Witness where of I have hereunto Sett my hand and Seal this Twenty Second day of September In the Year of our Lord One thousand Seven Hundred and forty One – 1741

# APPENDIX 4

## READING FURNACE—A BRIEF HISTORY, 1736/7-1783

*"A road was laid out from the Coventry Iron Works on the French Creek to the town of Lancaster aforesaid to the said to the Iron Works, forking the said Road near the Plantation of Widow Roberts, to lead to a new Furnace on the said Creek called Redding's Furnace..."*

PROVINCIAL COUNCIL MEETING, JANRY. 4TH, 1738

About 1736, prior to Nutt's death and while keeping his interests in the Coventry Iron-Works, William Branson decided to build a separate furnace. He built it on a 745-acre tract west of Coventry in Nantmeal on the South Branch of the French Creek. He had purchased the tract by deed dated February 28, 1723. This expansion was protentially the result of the two partner's disagreements or just Branson wanting to have his own furnace. Samuel Nutt was not involved in its management although Branson appears to have initially used the Coventry refinery forge and the company's distribution network. The furnace, which had a number of spellings, eventually became Reading Furnace.

The furnace is easily dated by two road petitions; one showing that it was being built and the other showing that it had been built. Reading Furnace was begun in 1736 and was still "errecting" in January of 1737. It is assumed that its first blast was in 1737. The furnace construction is mentioned in Council Meeting records January 25th, 1737:

"A Petition of sundry Inhabitants of Lancaster was read at a Council Meeting held in Philadelphia on January 25, 1737 requesting a road from the town of Lancaster to the Coventry Iron Works, on French Creek. One branch of said road was to goe to the new Furnace, called Redding's Furnace, now errecting on said Creek."

Branson, who was born near Reading, England, apparently picked the name from there. This furnace has a separate history from the Coventry Works although it is often mingled and confused with Warwick Furnace which was built the following year and was also located on the South Branch. In 1986, local historian, Estellle Cremers wrote a definitive history of the site entitled, *Reading Furnace 1736*. There was some early confusion between the Reading Furnace on French Creek and the Nutt/Branson furnace on Rock Run at Coventry also named Redding. Isabella Batchelder in the 1874 *Potts Memorial* quotes an unnamed document providing the following: "The 15th day of March, 1736, Samuel Nutt and William Bronson entered into an agreement with John Potts to carry on their furnace called Redding, recently built near Coventry, and of which they are styled "joint owners."

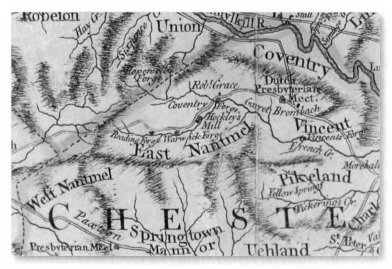

*London, Printed for Robt. Sayer & J. Bennett, 1775*
*Showing Coventry, Reading and Warwick*

As mentioned, Nutt's death did not dissolve the French Creek Iron-Works management. Between 1737 and 1740, Branson operated Reading under an Agreement of Co-partnership with the Nutt heirs. He supplied a specified amount of pig iron to Coventry Forge and the Reading, Warwick and Coventry works and assumed responsibility for a portion of each others debts. Almost immediately though, Branson was making stoves at Reading. He sold a stove to Benjamin Franklin on January 14, 1738, and on November 15, 1738. In 1739, he offered that: "one can purchase from him in Philadelphia: several kinds of iron stoves, also single plates." He indicated they could be obtained at the "new city" of Lancaster, at Harris Ferry, and at the "so called Reading Furnace, where they are cast."

Reading used the French Creek Mine's iron ore. Branson notes in his 1741 suit against Nutt's heirs that he owned one-half. Branson hired on-site managers to run the furnace, including his sons-in-law. He purchased the old Jenkins Forge in Lancaster County and changed the name to Windsor Forge. The furnace was active up until the Revolutionary War when it was being rented out. James Old, the ironmaster at that time, made cannon for the Continental Service there. It was used as an encampment by Washington's Army in September of 1777. It was closed about that time, and the Potts and Rutter interests at Warwick purchased much of the timberland. In 1783, Hermelin indicated that: "The Reading blast furnace in Chester County, abandoned partly because their own forests are used up by coaling, and partly because their ore has become too expensive." Branson's grandson, Samuel Vanleer (1747-1825), purchased the furnace tract from the other heirs and after the Revolution built Reading Forge on the furnace site.

# APPENDIX 5

## WARWICK FURNACE—A BRIEF HISTORY, 1738-1867

*Item. I likewise give unto her [Anna Nutt] One hundred & twenty acres of Land on the North side of the South Branch of the French Creek in Such a place as she shall think proper to Build a Furnace on, Provided it be not above one hundred and thirty Perches in Length upon the said Creek and to her Heirs, with Liberty to Cut as much Timber of the adjacent Land as Build the same.*

1737 WILL OF SAMUEL NUTT

It is generally accepted that Samuel Nutt decided to build his own furnace without his partner because Branson built Reading Furnace. Nutt lived to see the furnace started, but was deceased before its first blast. Nutt's wife Anna is often given credit for building the furnace, but it was built by some combination of herself, Samuel Nutt, Jr. and her son, Samuel Savage. Samuel Nutt, Sr.'s estate accounting taken the 24th and 25th of May 1738 shows that Warwick was being built at that time: "650 Acres Land in Nanmill on where the New Furnace is building with Sundry out Houses." A value of £525 was placed on the property.

Warwick Furnace was built on the 650-acre tract Nutt warranted and surveyed to him May 2, 1719. It was located in northern Chester County in East Nantmeal Township (now Warwick Township) on the

South Branch of French Creek between Coventry Forge and Reading Furnaces. It was about 19 miles southeast from "Readingtown," 7 miles south of Pottsgrove, and two miles from the Nutt's iron ore tract.

The younger Samuel Nutt ran Warwick briefly but died intestate in 1739. The widows Anna (Rutter) Savage Nutt and her daughter Rebecca (Savage) Nutt were involved in managing the furnace as joint owners. By September 1739, Anna and Rebecca Nutt were sending pig iron to Philadelphia.

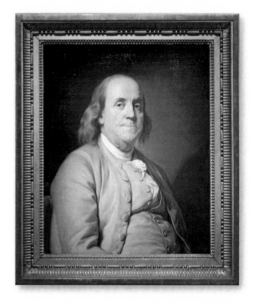

In 1740, Anna Nutt gave one-fifth of the furnace from her one-half share to son Samuel Savage (1707-1742) and for the next several years, the furnace was run under Samuel Savage & Co. Savage died in 1742. After Savage's death, several shareholders were involved in its management. Savage's widow married ironmaster George Taylor (1716-1784) who was involved in production at both Warwick and Coventry Forge. In 1740, Robert Grace (1709-1766) married the widow Rebecca Nutt, and represented her interests in the partnership and managed the operation. In 1742, Benjamin Franklin, a friend of Grace, gave him the model of an open stove (given the name Franklin stove).

In December of 1741, John Potts signed an agreement with Robert Grace to rent his half of the furnace. The agreement also stated that Potts would produce Franklin stoves. Warwick became the largest producer of Franklin Stoves in the state. John Potts (1710-1768), was the husband of Anna Nutt's daughter Ruth and at that time took over the management of Warwick from Grace, who then concentrated on Coventry Iron Works. By the mid-1740s, Potts was also renting Savage's portion. Both Warwick and Coventry were run under the firm of

Grace & Potts. John Potts also reopened Rock Run at Coventry. During the 1750s, Potts built Warwick into one of the largest charcoal iron furnaces in Pennsylvania making it the "king-pin" for his iron empire. Potts eventually obtained a three-eights ownership.

During the 1760s, Potts rented out the furnace to a series of companies comprised of his sons Thomas (1735-1785), Samuel (1736-1793), and John (1738-c.1790) and each managed it for a time. Son Thomas obtained one-half ownership from the Graces, who were his in-laws, as well as all of Coventry Works property. At John Potts, Sr.'s death in 1768, son John consolidated ownership and ran the furnace until 1770 when he sold it to his brother Samuel. In 1771, brother-in-law Thomas Rutter (1732-1795) purchased one-half from Samuel and it was this partnership that ran it during the Revolution until the 1790s.

The partners contracted with the Pennsylvania government in 1775 to make cannon and other armaments. Warwick is also mentioned on Knox's Estimate of Ammunition showing munitions were made there throughout the war. In September 1777, the American Army camped in the French Creek Valley at Reading and Warwick Furnaces. During the war, Potts & Rutter purchased the lands belonging to Branson's old non-operating Reading Furnace in Chester County, which closed in 1778. Samuel Hermelin mentioned Warwick in 1783 as producing 900 tons annually.

After the Revolution, Potts and Rutter started investing in anthracite coal lands in what was then upper Berks County. Needing capital, Samuel sold one-fourth of his interest in the furnace to Ironmaster Thomas Mayburry (1740-1797), which was eventually purchased back, and to Ironmaster Thomas May (1731-1792) another fourth, who retained it until his death. Warwick is shown as active and producing 1,200 tons annually on Samuel Potts' 1789 list, the highest production in Pennsylvania. Thomas May died in 1792, Samuel Potts in 1793 and Thomas Rutter in 1795, and there was a court fight as to whether the Rutter or Potts heirs would obtain a majority interest and run it. The Potts family "won" and Samuel's son, David Potts (c.1762-1832), who was the manager of Joanna Furnace, Berks County, became manager. David's son,

David Potts, Jr. (c.1794-1863), who also served as a U.S. Congressman, ran it until the 1860s. In 1826, David, Samuel and Joanna Potts sold one-fifth of the furnace and one-fourth of the lands to David and Reese Evans, but David Potts retained management.

Warwick declined after the Civil War because it was too far from markets. Thomas May Potts (1797-1876), and brother Nathaniel Potts (1798-1873), who took over after David's death, closed Warwick in 1867, and began selling some of the lands associated with the furnace. After Thomas May Potts' death in 1876, the property was left to three nephews who continued selling off part of the acreage and sold 550 acres and the furnace tract to Thomas K. Sterrett for $17,500. He operated the saw and gristmill and apparently a forge, which was named in a suit brought against him in 1886 by neighbor B. F. James. James complained that after Sterrett rebuilt the dam, that it held water back from James' property. There is no mention of iron production after this time.

# APPENDIX 6

## COVENTRY FORGE—A BRIEF HISTORY, 1722-1860

While the furnace at the French Creek Iron-Works closed around 1747, the forge, named Coventry Forge, had a long existence and numerous owners. Coventry received iron from Warwick and initially from Reading Furnace. Coventry Forge is listed on Gov. William Denny's list of 1757 as producing 339 tons in seven years (which was one of the lower amounts). Coventry is shown as "Robert Grace" on Scull's 1759 map; but both Grace and Coventry are listed separately on William Scull's 1770 map.

In 1764, the Graces sold to their son-in-law Thomas Potts (1735-1785) their one-half interest in the works. Thomas' father, John Potts, owned Anna Nutt's portion by that time. Samuel Savage's portion had been obtained by the Hockley family. Although the Coventry steel furnace appears not to have been in operation at the time of the sale, it was reopened by Thomas and his brothers Samuel and John, under the firm of Thomas Potts & Co. Steel was produced there through the Revolution.

Thomas managed and paid taxes on the works from 1764 to 1783 except during the war years of 1775-1778 when it was apparently inactive. In 1779, and 1780, Potts was taxed for a steel furnace, and in 1781 for two forges. When Hermelin wrote his *Report on the Mines* in 1783, he noted "Coventry or Potts Forge, 1 hammer, 3 furnaces, d.o. [pig iron] 120 tons…At Coventry there is one blister steel furnace with two pipes." Schoepf visited in November of 1783 and noted there were three hearths and three hammers: "The hammers lie parallel with the shaft… The bellows are of wood, and consist of two cylindrical casks, fitting closely the one into the other..."

Samuel Hodgdon's letter book for May 1780 shows Potts was sent bar iron by the "Government" to make steel for the war effort and his estate inventory notes he had a contract for same with the "American government." Thomas Potts died in 1785 and brother Jesse Potts (1756-1814) paid taxes on the property that year although it is unclear if he was running it. The works were rented in 1786/87 to Ellis Jones & Co., (Jones, Thomas Bull, John Smith, and Samuel Potts) and from 1787/90 to George North & John Evans. North & Evans, who were brothers-in-law, ended their partnership in 1790, but Coventry forgeman Philip Benner (1762-1832) stayed on for two years at which time he removed to Centre County, where he took Coventry workers with him. Coventry is shown as active on Samuel Potts' 1789 list. Thomas Potts' son-in-law, Robert May (1750-1812) purchased the forge tract in 1792 and ran it until 1796 when he sold the property to Jonathan Hudson and Thomas Church. Between 1792 and 1812, Coventry's pig iron was received from Joanna Furnace. Church & Hudson sold the forge the following year to Thomas Davis who sold it in 1807 to George Christman, whose family operated it, or leased it, on-and-off until the mid-1800s.

Coventry Forge is listed by Peter Lesley in 1859 as still active, having eight forge fires and one hammer powered by water, having produced 352 tons of blooms in 1855. Leslie notes it was owned by George Christman of Pughtown and leased to J. Bingham.

# BIBLIOGRAPHY

## COUNTY DOCUMENTS

Chester County, Pennsylvania
  Deed Books
  Road Dockets, Court of Quarter Sessions
  Tax Assessments and Returns
  Wills and Administrations
New Castle County, Delaware
  Deed Books
Philadelphia County, Pennsylvania
  Wills and Administrations

## MANUSCRIPTS/PRIMARY DOCUMENTS/GENERAL COLLECTIONS

Besse, Joseph,  A Brief Account Of Many of the Prosecutions of the People call'd Quakers in the Exchequer, Ecclesiastical And Other Courts, for Demands Recoverable by the Acts made in the 7th and 8th in the Reign of King William the Third, for the more Easy Recovery of Tithes, Church-Rates, E&t, Printed and Sold by the Assign of J. Sowle, at the Bible in George-Yard, Lombard -street, London, 1736.

Bucks County Historical Society
  Receipts from Proprietary to Samuel Nutt for surveys and quit rents
  Warwick Furnace Material in General Collection, folder 149

Chester County, Pennsylvania, Record of the Courts, "Enterys of the Orphans Court of Chester County, 1716-1730", Vol. III.

Chester County Historical Society

Nutt, Samuel, *Savorall Rare Sacrets and Choyce Curiossityes*, Unpublished Memorandum Book, 1702.

Churchman, John, *An account of the Gospel labours, and Christian Experiences of a Faithful Minister of Christ, John Churchman, Late of Nottingham in Pennsylvania, deceased*, James Philips printer, Philadelphia and London, 1731.

Colonial Records

Vol. IV

Commissions Issued by the Province of Pennsylvania

*Enterys of the Orphans Court of Chester County, Pennsylvania, 1716-1730, 1732-1734*, Transcribed by Miss Dorothy B. Lapp, Published by Richard T. and Mildred C. Williams, Danboro, Pennsylvania, 1973.

Historical Society of Pennsylvania

    Forges and Furnaces Collection 212

      Coventry Forge Account Book 1727-1733

      Coventry Forge Account Book, 1746-1754

      Coventry Forge Ledger B, 1727-1730

      Coventry Forge Ledger, 1730-1732

      Coventry Forge Ledger, 1732-1733

      Coventry Forge Ledger, 1734-1740

      Coventry Forge Ledger F, 1736-1741

      Coventry Forge Ledger, 1742-1748

      Coventry Forge Ledger, 1745-1748

    Jonathan Dickinson Letter Book 1715-1721

    Jacob and Isaac Taylor Papers

Kalm, Peter, *Travels in North America*, Benson, Adolph B., Editor, Dover Publications, New York, 1964.

Lancaster County Historical Society

*Laws of the Commonwealth of Pennsylvania*, J, Bioren for Carey, Matthew, Philadelphia, 1803.

Library Company of Philadelphia

Library of Congress

    American Memory - Maps

Minutes of the Board of Property, Vol. 1, Minute book G, Harrisburg, 1893.

Minutes of the Provincial Council of Pennsylvania

Mittelberger, Gottlieb, *Journey to Pennsylvania in the Year 1750*, Translated by E.J. Eben, Philadelphia, 1898.

Pennsylvania Archives

    2nd Series

    3rd Series

Pennsylvania State Archives, Harrisburg, PA

    Land Records Survey Books

    Letters of Attorney

    Original Purchases Register, 1682-1762

    Records of the Land Office

    Rock Run Furnace Account Book 1743

Pennsylvania Warrant Register

Pottsgrove Manor

    Transcript of Indenture, between Samuel Nutt and Israel Taylor, dated December 2, 1720

Pottstown Historical Society

    General Collection

Schoepf, Johann David, Morrison, Alfred J., Editor, *Travels in the Confederation, 1783-1784, from the German of Johann David Schoepf*, J. W. Campbell, Philadelphia, Pennsylvania, 1911.

*The Statutes at Large from Pennsylvania from 1682 to 1801*, Wm. Stanley Ray, Harrisburg, 1899, Vol. VI.

Swarthmore Friends Historical Library

    Concord Meeting Records

*Votes and Proceedings of the House of Representatives of the Province of Pennsylvania, Beginning Fourteenth Day of October, 1767*, Printed and Sold by Henry Miller, Sixth Volume, Philadelphia, 1776.

## MAPS

British Spy Map of Southeastern Pennsylvania from the Susquehanna to the Delaware River, 1777

Holme, Thomas, "A mapp of ye improved part of Pensilvania in America, divided into countyes, townships and lotts, 1687"

Lotter, Tobias Conrad, "Pensylvania, Nova Jersey et Nova York cum regionibus ad Fluvium Delaware in America sitis," Augsburg, Germany, c1748.

Map of Pennsylvania, Printed for Robt. Sayer & J. Bennett, 1775, London.

Scull, Nicholas "To the Honourable Thomas Penn and Richard Penn, Esqrs., true & absolute proprietaries & Governours of the Province of Pennsylvania & counties of New-Castle, Kent & Sussex on Delaware this map of the improved part of the Province of Pennsylvania," Philadelphia, 1759.

Scull, William, "To the Honorable Thomas Penn and Richard Penn, Esquires, true and absolute proprietaries and Governors of the Province of Pennsylvania and the territories thereunto belonging and to the Honorable John Penn, Esquire, Lieutenant-Governor of the same, this map. Of the Province of Pennsylvania." 1770.

## NEWSPAPERS/MAGAZINES/ALMANACS

*American Weekly Mercury* (Philadelphia)

*New York Gazette*

*Pennsylvania Gazette* (Philadelphia)

*Reading Eagle,* February 7, 1916, and April 30, 1916, "Coventry Forge and Its Founder; Sam. Nutt, Famous as "Iron King."

*Sower's Almanac*

## ARTICLES/PAPERS/NEWSLETTERS

*American-German Review*
    Russell W. Gilbert, "Sower's Almanac as an Advertising Medium," Vol. XV, October 1948, Number 1.

*Bulletin of the Historical Society of Montgomery County*
    Graham, Daniel A., "The Location and Use of Original Pennsylvania Forge and Furnace Books," Vol. XXXIV, No. 1, 2004.

Carnegie Institution of Washington
    *Proceedings and Debates of the British Parliaments Respecting North America: 1728-1739*, Vol. 338, 1939.

*Early American Life*
    Handler, Mimi, "A Restoration on French Creek," Vol. 33, February 2002.

National Park Service
> National Register of Historic Places, Bennett, Margaret, Busenkill, Mary, Cremers, Estelle, Jackson, David J., Miller, Elizabeth, Morris, Eleanor, M., Murphy, J. Kelly, "Coventryville Historic District," Washington, DC, 1977.

*New England Historical and Genealogical Register*
> Samuel Shackford, "The Lineage of Abraham Lincoln Traced from Samuel Lincoln," Vol. 41, April, 1887.

*Pennsylvania History*
> Bezis-Selfa, John, "Slavery and the Disciplining of Free Labor in the Colonial Mid-Atlantic Iron Industry," Empire, Society and Labor, Vol. 64, 1997.

*Pennsylvania Magazine of History and Biography*
> Sheeder, Frederick, "East Vincent Township, Chester County Pennsylvania," Vol. 34, 1910.
> Pennypacker, Samuel W., "Joseph Richardson's Road," Vol. 35, 1911.

*The Perkiomen Region*
> "Pig Iron Marketed in 1738-'39," Volumes I, II, and III, September 1894 to April 1901.

*The Sabbath Recorder*
> Charles H. Green, "Samuel Nutt," Vol. 78, No. 19, May 10, 1915.

## BOOKS

Acrelius, Israel, *History of New Sweden*, Historical Society of Pennsylvania, Reynolds, William M., Editor, Philadelphia, 1874.

Bezis-Selfa, John, *Forging America: Ironworkers and Adventurers in the Industrial Revolution*, Cornell University, 2004.

Bining, Arthur Cecil, *British Regulation of the American Iron Industry*, A.M. Kelly, 1933.

_____, *Pennsylvania Iron Manufacture in the Eighteenth Century*, Pennsylvania History and Museum Commission, Harrisburg, Pennsylvania, 1987.

Bishop, John Leander, Freedley, Edwin Troxell, and Young, Edward. *A History of American Manufactures from 1608 to 1860*, Vol. 1, Published by E. Young, 1866.

Brody, Susannah, "Samuel Nutt," *Prosperous Beginnings, Chester County Biographies*, Chester County Historical Society, 1999.

Buck, William Joseph, *William Penn in America*, Friends Book Association, Philadelphia, 1883.

Carter, Jane Levis. *Edgemont, The Story of a Township*, KNA Press Inc., Kennett Square, PA, 1976.

Chalkley, Thomas, *A Collection of the Works of that Ancient, Faithful Servant of Jesus Christ, Thomas Chalkley*, 5th Edition, James Philips Printer, London, M,DCC,XCI.

Clegg, Miriam, *The Nail Factory, Phoenixville Chester County, PA*, The Historical Society of the Phoenixville Area, 1981.

Colonial Dames of America, *Forges and Furnaces in the Province of Pennsylvania*, Printed for the Society, Philadelphia, 1914.

Cope, Gilbert, *Genealogy of the Dunwoody and Hood Families*, Tribune Printing Company, 1899.

Cope, Gilbert and Ashmead, Henry Graham, *Historic Homes and Institutions and Genealogical and Personal Memoirs of Chester and Delaware Counties*, Lewis Publishing Co., Vol. 1, 1904.

Cremers, Estelle, *Coventry the Skool Kill District A Brief History of the Three Coventry Townships 1700-1850*, Masthof Press, Morgantown, Pa, 2003.

———, *Reading Furnace 1736*, Reading Furnace Press, Elverson, PA 1986.

———, *30,000 Acres Vincent and Pikeland Townships 1686-1856*, Privately Printed, 1989.

———, *Treasures of the Upper French Creek Valley – Story of Warwick Township*, Olde Springfield Shoppe, Elverson, PA, 1982.

Duffin, James M., *Guide to the Mortgages of the General Loan Office of the Province of Pennsylvania, 1724-1756*, Genealogical Society of Pennsylvania, Monograph Series no. 1, 1995.

Egle, William Henry, *History of the Commonwealth of Pennsylvania: Civil, Political and Military*, E. M. Gardner, Philadelphia, 1883.

Ellis, Franklin and Evans, Samuel, *History of Lancaster County Pennsylvania*, Everts & Peck, Philadelphia, 1883.

Franklin, Benjamin, *Memoirs of the Life and Writings of Benjamin Franklin*, Henry Colburn, London, 1818.

Furthey, J. Smith, and Cope, Gilbert, *History of Chester County Pennsylvania*, Louis H. Everts, Philadelphia, 1881.

*Geology of Chester County*, J. Peter Leslie, Editor, Board of Commissioners, Harrisburg, PA, 1883.

Graham, Daniel A., *Early Charcoal Iron Forges, Furnaces, and Slitting Mills in Chester County Pennsylvania, 1718-1830: Including Sketches on the Works and a Finding Aid for the Original Forge and Furnace Books at the Chester County Historical Society*, Ellicott City, MD, December 2006.

_____, *Colebrook Dale Furnace (1720-1770) and Pine Forge (1720-1844): Pennsylvania's First Blast Furnace and Refinery Forge*, Montrose, PA, September 2010.

_____, *Colonial Pennsylvania Cast Iron Fire Backs, Stove Plates, and Warming Stoves 1726-1760*, County of Montgomery, Pottsgrove Manor Historical Site, Pottstown, PA, 2012.

_____, *Thomas Rutter I (c1660-1730) of Germantown, Pennsylvania and the Birth of the Pennsylvania Iron Industry*, Ellicott City, MD, August 1996.

_____, *Samuel Savage Sr. (c1655-1707), Stonemason, and his Descendants of Philadelphia, Berks and Chester Counties, Pennsylvania, through four Generations*, Ellicott City, MD, January 2004.

Hermelin, Samuel Gustaf, *Report About the Mines in the United States of America, 1783;* translated from the Swedish with introduction and notes by Amandus Johnson, Published by John Morton Memorial Museum, Philadelphia, 1931.

Horle, Craig W. (et. al.), "Samuel Nutt," *Lawmaking and Legislators in Pennsylvania: a Biographical Dictionary*, Center for Public Policy, Temple University, University of Pennsylvania Press, Philadelphia, Vol. II, 1710-1756, 1997.

Huston, Charles, *An Essay on the History and Nature of Original Titles to Land in the Province and State of Pennsylvania*, T.&J.W. Johnson, Printers, Philadelphia, 1849.

James, Mrs. Thomas Potts (Isabella Batchelder), *The Memorial of Thomas Potts Junior*, privately printed, Cambridge, Massachusetts, 1874.

Jenkins, Howard M., *Pennsylvania Colonial and Federal: a History, 1608-1903*, Pennsylvania Historical Publishing Association, Vol. 3, 1903.

Landis, James C., *Will the Real Mary Lincoln Please Stand Up?*, Private Printing, 1996.

Learned, Marion Dexter, *Abraham Lincoln, an American Migration*, William J. Campbell, Philadelphia, 1909.

Leslie, J. Peter, *The Iron Manufacturers Guide to the Furnaces, Forges and Rolling Mills of the United States*, John Wiley, Publisher, New York, 1859.

Lemay, L.A. Leo, *The Life of Benjamin Franklin*, Vol. 2, Printer and Publisher, 1730-1747, University of Pennsylvania Press, Philadelphia, 2006, "The Franklin Stove."

Loomis, Betty K., Philips, Ada P., *The Forgers of Coventryville, Knauertown, St. Peters, Warwick*, West Chester, Pennsylvania: Project 1776, West Chester, PA 2016.

MacEltree, Wilmer, *Around the Boundaries of Chester County*, Privately Printed, West Chester, PA, 1934.

McCleskey, Turk, *The Road to Black Ned's Forge*, University of Virginia Press, Charlottesville, VA, 2014.

Mercer, Henry, *The Bible in Iron (or Pictured Stoves and Stove Plates of the Pennsylvania Germans)*, Bucks County Historical Society, Doylestown, PA, 1914 edition.

Pearse, John B., *A Concise History of the Iron Manufacture of the American Colonies up to the Revolution and of Pennsylvania up to the Present*, Burt Franklin, New York, 1972, reprint of the 1876 edition.

Pennypacker, Samuel Whitaker, *Pennsylvania, The Keystone, a Short History*, Christopher Sower Co., Philadelphia, 1914.

Rogers, Albert N., *Seventh Day Baptists in Europe and America*, Vol. II, American Tract Society, Plainfield, NJ, 1910.

Scharf, J. Thomas, *History of Delaware, 1609-1888*, L.J. Richards, Philadelphia, 1888.

Scharf, John Thomas and Westcott, Thompson, *History of Philadelphia*, 1609-1884, L.H. Everts & Co., Philadelphia, 1884.

Schoel, Doris R. and Schoel, Meredith Fuller, *Message by Horseback*, 2007.

Sloto, Ronald, *Mines and Minerals of Chester County, Pennsylvania*, CreateSpace Independent Publishing Platform, 2016.

Smith, Lawrence Lowe, *Magnetite Deposits of French Creek, Pennsylvania*, Department of Internal Affairs, Topographic and Geologic Survey, 1931.

Swank, James M., *The American Iron Trade in 1876,* The American Iron and Steel Association, Philadelphia, 1876.

_____., *The History of the Manufacture of Iron in All Ages*, published by the author, Philadelphia, 1884.

Swedenborg, Emanuel, *Regnum Subterraneum Sive Minerale  De Ferro*, Dresden and Lipsec, Vol. II, 1734.

Thompson, William W., *Chester County and its People*, The Union History Company, Chicago and New York, 1898.

Weaver, William Woys, *The Christmas Cook -- Three Centuries of American Yuletide Sweets*, Harper Perennial, 1990.

White, William, *Friends in Warwickshire, in the 17th and 18th Centuries*, published by White and Pike, Birmingham, England, 1873.

# ENDNOTES

1 Both the 1997 *Lawmaking & Legislators of Pennsylvania* (LLP) and Estelle Cremers' 2003 *Coventry the Skool Kill District* attempted to present information on Nutt's ancestry. LLP indicates that a Samuel Nutt was baptized at Nuneaton, Warwickshire, about eight miles from Coventry, in October 1685. It notes no connection has been established of that Samuel Nutt to Samuel Nutt, the iron maker, but it does indicate a Robert Nutt of Nuneaton, a tallow-chandler, was presented at Warwickshire Quarter Sessions in 1683 and 1684 for illegally following the trade of ironmonger.

Cremers, who also discussed the Nuneaton connection, indicated that the baptized Samuel Nutt's parents are listed in the parish registers as Joseph and Elizabeth Nutt of Nuneaton. Joseph Nutt's 1701 will indicates that he was a wheelwright and had a young son named Samuel. Again, however, no connection to this family has been made and Nutt's antecedents remain unknown.

2 Mrs. Thomas Potts James (hereafter given as Isabella Batchelder), *The Memorial of Thomas Potts Junior*, privately printed, Cambridge, Massachusetts, 1874 (hereafter the *Potts Memorial*). Batchelder is basing this on a coat of arms she had access to, "Another coat of arms was found in Samuel Nutt's personal book, currently located at the Chester County Historical Society. The two coats of arms are similar, but Nutt lists under his: 'Sir Thomas Nutt of Lewis in The County Sussex.'" See Samuel Nutt, *Savorall Rare Sacrets and Choyce Curiossityes*, Unpublished Memorandum Book, Chester County Historical Society, Pennsylvania, 1702.

3 Samuel Nutt bequeathed 150 pounds Pennsylvania currency to both his well beloved friend "John Blaufoy of Eversham in Worchester Sheer" and to the heirs of Thomas Crook of Hay Park in York Shire.

4 William White, *Friends in Warwickshire, in the 17th and 18th Centuries*, published by White and Pike, Birmingham, England, 1873, pp. 50 and 122. White only lists some highlights of Meeting records. One gets the sense that if you reviewed Coventry Meeting records for the late 1600s and early 1700s you could uncover more on Samuel Nutt.

5 Joseph Besse, *A Brief Account of Many of the Prosecutions of the People call'd Quakers in the Exchequer, Ecclesiastical And Other Courts, for Demands Recoverable by the Acts made in the 7th and 8th in the Reign of King William the Third, for the more Easy Recovery of Tithes, Church-Rates, E&t*, Printed and sold by the Assign of J. Sowle, at the Bible in George-Yard, Lombard-street, London, 1736, p. 144. Besse's various works documented the persecution of Quakers in the 17th and 18th centuries in England.

6   Original Purchases Register, 1682-1762, Series 17.83, William Pardoe; and also, *Chester County Deed Book K, Vol. 10*, pp. 241-245. This was the 1,250 acres of land granted to Wm Pardoe by William Penn in 1681, but later assigned to Jno. Weight of Worchester who died and was given to his daughter Sarah Weight and her brother (unnamed). See Board of Property Meeting Records, 2mo, 10th, 1707. Minutes of the Board of Property, Vol. 1, Minute book G, Harrisburg, 1893, p. 484.

Cremers indicates that this land was surveyed and patented for him in Sadsbury Township and that some of which was still in possession when his estate was settled. This appears incorrect as it is not mentioned in his estate accounting. Nutt sold 400 acres of the Sadsbury land in 1720, and 425 acres in 1725. This leaves 325 acres unaccounted for. The only land mentioned in his estate that was not listed as in Coventry or Nantmeal was an unspecified sixty-four acre plot that is listed either as in Coventry on the estate accounting of Samuel Nutt, Jr. in 1739. However, the 1720 indenture selling the first 400 acres of land indicates Sarah Weight (mentioned in Board of Property Minutes) had land next to Nutt's. Perhaps, Nutt sold some of the land back to Sarah Weight.

7   Transcript of Indenture, between Samuel Nutt and Israel Taylor, dated December 2, 1720, Pottsgrove Manor. The indenture was recorded 16 May 1721, at Chester County (D4:175). Nutt also sold 425 acres of this land in 1725 shortly before he invested in Abington Furnace in Delaware.

8   Concord Meeting Records, Swarthmore Historical Friends Library.

9   Nutt's book currently resides at the Chester County Historical Society. See William Woys Weaver's transcription, *Savorall Rare Sacrets and Choyce Curiossityes*, Unpublished Memorandum Book, Chester County Historical Society, 1702-3. Of interest, many of the recipes have been copied and republished and it is noted as one of the first cookbooks in America. See *The Christmas Cook—Three Centuries of American Yuletide Sweets*, Harper Perennial, 1990.

10   Existing sources during the three-year period after immigration and before he settled on the French Creek tract are silent as to his whereabouts. His certificate at Concord Meeting was recorded 10th month (December) 1714. Nothing has been uncovered to show Nutt ever developed or even lived on the Sadsbury property.

11   Israel Acrelius (1714-1800) is quoted several times in this document. He was a Swede and an ordained minister of the Swedish Lutheran church. He went to Wilmington, Delaware, in 1749 (eleven years after Nutt had died) and was pastor of a congregation there. He returned to Sweden in 1756 and published his history in 1759. As a Swede, he had both an interest in the early Swedish settlement in Pennsylvania and an interest in iron making. He mentions Nutt, the ironworks and the mine, although by that time, Nutt was deceased and the French Creek Ironworks were already closed. It is unknown where he obtained his information.

12   For more information on Thomas Rutter and the founding of the Pennsylvania iron industry see Graham's *Thomas Rutter I (c1660-1730) of Germantown, Pennsylvania and the Birth of the Pennsylvania Iron Industry*; Ellicott City, MD, August 1996; and *Cole-*

*brook Dale Furnace (1720-1770) and Pine Forge (1720-1844). Pennsylvania's First Blast Furnace and Refinery Forge*, Montrose, PA, September, 2010.

13 *Jonathan Dickinson Letter Book 1715-1721*, Historical Society of Pennsylvania, p. 111. This letter book is a primary source of documentation on the early Pennsylvania iron industry. Although hard to read (most vowels look alike), Dickinson had an interest in what was going on up the Schuylkill River and reported on it.

14 *Pennsylvania State Archives, Land Records, Old Rights Index Bucks and Chester County.* French Creek was shown as Vincent River on Holmes' 1683 map of Pennsylvania. It is listed as such in several early documents where it is also given as Friends Creek. Some speculation has been espoused that French Creek is a derivation of Friends Creek.

15 Samuel Whitaker Pennypacker, *Pennsylvania, The Keystone, a Short History*, Christopher Sower Co., Philadelphia, 1914, p. 234. Pennypacker, who seems to have first recorded the story, and may be the originator of it, put it in a 1911 article in the *Pennsylvania Magazine of History and Biography,* entitled "Joseph Richardson's Road." Of interest, the 1914 *Forges and Furnaces of the Province of Pennsylvania*, which repeats the story in their section on Coventry Forge, indicates that information was taken from the *Coventry Ledger, Book B.* No page number is given.

16 *Pennsylvania State Archives, Old Rights Index, Bucks and Chester Counties, Series 17.78, Survey Book D, Vol. 74*, p. 152. The September 18, 1717, warrant date and the patent date are found in *Patent Book A, No. 6*, page 9. The March 16, 1718, survey is found in *Survey Book D, Vol. 74*, p. 150.

17 *Pennsylvania State Archives, Land Records, Survey Book D-74-150.* The Warrant, Survey (A-18-175) and Return of Survey and Patent (A-6-9) are on file at the Pennsylvania Archives. For the Board's Minutes, see William Henry Egle, *Minutes of the Board of Property of the Province of Pennsylvania, Pennsylvania Archives, 2nd Series, Vol. 14*, Harrisburg, 1890, p. 620. The August 20th, 1720, date is also recited in the Articles of Agreement dated February 28, 1724, when Nutt sold 1/3 of six acres, "being the iron mine" to each of his partners.

18 The patent for the 250-acre ore tract and the 650-acre Warwick tract was signed by Thomas and Richard Penn July 5, 1736, and is on microfilm at the Pennsylvania State Archives.

19 Bucks County Historical Society, MSC 149, Folder 1, Item 4, Receipts for Payment of Surveys, Warwick Furnace.

20 *Pennsylvania State Archives, Land Records, Survey Book, A-18-173.*

21 *Records of the Land Office, Record Group 17, Letters of Attorney, Book D, #2*, pp. 376-380.

22 *Peter Kalm's Travels in North America, the English Version of 1770*, Dover Publishing, 1987, p. 159.

23   Israel Acrelius, *History of New Sweden*, William M. Reynolds, Editor Historical Society of Pennsylvania, Philadelphia, 1874, p. 165.

24   Wilber MacEltree, *Around the Boundaries of Chester County*, Privately Printed, West Chester, PA, 1934, p. 518.

25   Samuel Gustaf Hermelin, *Report About the Mines in the United States of America, 1783;* translated from the Swedish with introduction and notes by Amandus Johnson, published by John Morton Memorial Museum, Philadelphia, 1931, pp. 29 and 33-34.

26   Johann David Schoepf, *Travels in the Confederation*, Bergman Publishers, New York, 1968, Vol. II, p. 7.

27   *Rock Run Account Book 1743*, Pennsylvania Archives.

28   Bucks County Historical Society, MSC 149, Folder 1, Item 6, Inventory of the Horses, Carts, and Utensils belonging to Warwick Furnace taken this seventeenth day of December, 1741.

29   *Potts Memorial*, p. 49.

30   Wilber MacEltree, p. 94.

31   *Potts Memorial*, pp. 30-31.

32   *Minutes of the Board of Property*, EK Meyers, Printer, Harrisburg, 1893, *Vol. 1, Minute Book "H"*, p. 642. Also see *Survey Book A-18-174* and *D-78-300*.

33   The Old Rights for Chester County show that Samuel Nutt applied for warrants on three tracts of land: one for 250 acres, which became known as the mine tract, one for 400 acres, and one for 800 acres, of which 300 acres were originally surveyed. While several documents note that the forge was on the 400-acre warrant, both surveys returned for the 300 acres show the land that the forge was on. Perhaps the 400 and 300-acre warrants were combined.

34   The fact that Nutt was not shown as a resident until 1720 may indicate that the forge was not established until 1719 or 1720.

35   John Leander Bishop and Edwin Troxell Freedley, *A History of American Manufactures from 1608 to 1860,* Vol. 1, Published by E. Young, 1866, p. 552.

36   This supposition first appears in Bishop and Freedley. It was also used by James M. Swank, *The American Iron Trade in 1876,* The American Iron and Steel Association, Philadelphia, 1876, p. 127.

37   *Pennsylvania Archives, Third Series, Vol.1, Minutes of the Board of Property*, Charles M. Busch Printer, Harrisburg, 1894, *Minute Book "K"*, p. 75. See also *Patent Book A, No. 8*, page 2.

38  *Chester County, Pennsylvania, Record of the Courts, "Enterys of the Orphans Court of Chester County, 1716-1730", Vol. III*, pp. 20-21.

39  *Pennsylvania State Archives, Land Records, Survey Book, D-78-300.*

40  *Dickinson Letter Book, June 2, 1719*, p. 244.

41  J. Smith Furthey and Gilbert Cope, *History of Chester County Pennsylvania*, Louis H. Everts, Philadelphia, 1881, p. 344. Original found in the Jacob and Isaac Taylor Papers at the Historical Society of Pennsylvania, July 2, 1720, XIV, Document 2930.

42  The date Mordecai Lincoln entered into the partnership is unknown. It is routinely given as 1724/25 although this was the year he left. Lincoln was unquestionably at the forge by 1720 as he and Nutt are listed there on the tax roles. On the February 1725 Articles of Agreement selling Branson his share, it notes he helped build a dwelling house and forge. It is probable that when Nutt used the adjectives "we" and "our," he was including both Branson and Lincoln.

43  *Dickinson Letter Book*, pp. 240-241. See also Graham's *Colebrook Dale Furnace (1720-1770) and Pine Forge (1720-1844): Pennsylvania's First Blast Furnace and Refinery Forge*, Montrose, PA, September, 2010.

44  "Persons Admitted as Freemen to the City of Philadelphia, 1704-1720," *The Pennsylvania Genealogical Magazine*, Volume XXXIII , p. 96.

45  Turk McCleskey, *The Road to Black Ned's Forge*, University of Virginia Press, Charlottesville, VA, 2014, p. 232.

46  Furthey and Cope, p. 172.

47  Genevieve Tallman Arboga, *God Blew, and They Were Scattered: Peter's People* (New Frontiers), Book 3, p. 54, and Susan Stroud Robeson, *An Historical and Genealogical Account of Andrew Robeson*, L. B. Lippincott, Philadelphia, 1916. A later work, James C. Landis, *Will the Real Mary Lincoln Please Stand Up?*, 1996, Private Printing, indicates Mordecai married Mary Millard, the daughter of Thomas Millard not Mary Robeson.

48  *Records of the Land Office, Record Group 17, Letters of Attorney, Book D, #2*, p. 370.

49  I can find no warrant for Lincoln at the Archives during this time period and the articles may have been confusing it with the Nutt warrant. That said, Estelle Cremers indicates in her *Coventry The Skool Kill District* book on page 149, that Lincoln obtained a warrant in Coventry in 1722. Lincoln is listed as living on the 1/3 of the forge property, which he owned at that time.

50  MacEltree, p. 502.

51  Nutt signed Articles of Agreement with his two partners to sell each a "full equal third Part" of the land on which the forge and buildings were located. At the same time, he also sold 1/3 of six acres the ore mine to each. Three of these four documents selling the land are dated "February 28, 1723." The other document, which was filed first, is dated February 28, **1723/4**. It is assumed all the documents were signed in 1724, February being the 12th month in the Julian calendar and the "**/4**" was not added.

52  On 3 month, 7, 1724, George Dandesson requested a small parcel of land from the Land Commissioners 3 or 4 miles from Samuel Nutt, who recommended him as an honest man. *Board of Property of the Province of Pennsylvania*, Harrisburg, 1893, *Minute Book I*, p. 721.

53  *Records of the Land Office, Record Group 17, Letters of Attorney, Book D, #2*, pp. 376-379. This is the date for the 800-acre tract not the 300-acre tract and appears incorrect.

54  Frederick Sheeder, "East Vincent Township, Chester County, Pennsylvania," *Pennsylvania History*, Vol. 34, No. 1, 1910, p. 81.

55  *Potts Memorial*, p. 49.

56  MacEltree, p. 507.

57  Photograph by Jay Erb, Warwick County Park. Cyrus Fox in a 1916 article, John Ferris in his 1927 *Old Trails and Roads in Penn's Land*, and Wilber MacEltree in his 1936 book all reference this sign. MacEltree provides a facsimile. The sign was located in a barn at Warwick Park (2016) when the picture was taken. It has since been restored and installed at the Coventryville Access of Warwick Park, just south of Route 23 on Coventryville Rd.

58  The 650-acre tract, listed as "not improved," was mortgaged to the General Loan Office on July 7, 1736, by Samuel Nutt of Coventry Township, yeoman, for £99. See James M. Duffin, *Guide to the Mortgages of the General Loan Office of the Province of Pennsylvania, 1724-1756*, Genealogical Society of Pennsylvania, Monograph Series No. 1, 1995, p. 20.

59  *Votes and Proceedings of the House of Representatives of the Province of Pennsylvania*, Printed and Sold by B. Franklin and D. Hall, Philadelphia, Vol. II, 1753, p. 375. Of interest, the "signed and sealed certificate of the election for Chester County for 1724" showing Nutt's Assembly election, was on display at the 1907 Jamestown Exhibition.

60  *Votes and Proceedings of the House of Representatives of the Province of Pennsylvania*, Printed and Sold by B. Franklin and D. Hall, Philadelphia, Vol. III, 1754, p. 3. Nutt did not serve in the 1724 or the 1725 sessions as is often stated in numerous secondary sources. For an in-depth description of Nutt's Assembly votes and service, see *Lawmaking and Legislators in Pennsylvania: a Biographical Dictionary*, Vol. II, 1997.

61  *Pennsylvania Archives, 2nd Series, Vol. IX, Provincial Officers for the Three Original Counties*, p. 677.

62  *Records of the Land Office, Record Group 17, Letters of Attorney, Book D, #2*, pp. 380-381. See Samuel Shackford, "The Lineage of Abraham Lincoln Traced from Samuel Lincoln," *New England Historical and Genealogical Register*, Vol. 41, April 1887, p. 155. This was the first article that used this document. Shackford listed as his source: "A deed on file among the records of the department of internal affairs of Pennsylvania, Dec. 14th, 1725." The Department of Internal Affairs eventually became the Pennsylvania Archives in Harrisburg. Over the years, Shackford's information was presented in numerous documents with slightly different variations of spelling, capitalization and punctuation, but the Shackford publication seems to be the source of all of them. See also for another version, Marion Dexter Learned, *Abraham Lincoln, an American Migration*, William J. Campbell, Philadelphia, 1909, pp. 22-24.

63  *Records of the Land Office, Record Group 17, Letters of Attorney, Book D, #2*, p. 382.

64  *Votes and Proceedings of the House of Representatives of the Province of Pennsylvania*, Printed and Sold by B. Franklin and D. Hall, Philadelphia, Vol. II, 1753, p.462.

65  In should be noted here that in 1726, Thomas Rutter and Samuel Nutt were the only ironmasters in Pennsylvania. However, Branson, Lincoln and Colebrook Dale's shareholders were obviously concerned about the health of their investment, and could be considered "Persons concerned in the Iron Works." Investors were also involved in Abington Furnace built in Delaware in 1725 and Durham Furnace was built the following year.

66  James Hill Martin, *Martin's Bench and Bar of Philadelphia*, Rees Welsh & Co., Printers, Philadelphia, 1883, p. 159.

67  *Chester County Deed Book K, Vol. 10*, pp. 246-248.

68  *Delaware, New Castle County Deeds H*, 1:222-226. The earliest furnaces and forges did not seem to be named. They were simply called after the owner ("Rutter's Forge") or the stream ("forge at Manatawny"). It wasn't until later in the 18th century that ironmasters began naming their works after wives or the wives of investors. See Graham's "The Location and Use of Original Pennsylvania Forge and Furnace Books," *Bulletin of the Historical Society of Montgomery County*, Vol. XXXIV, No. 1, 2004. Abington Furnace was also called Christiana Furnace. The earliest Coventry Forge books have several annotations of receiving pig iron from Christeen Furnace. Using Mercer, Cremers speculated that Christeen was another name for Rock Run but this may or may not be correct. As investors, Nutt and Branson would have received their shares in pig iron.

69  For more information on the Savage family, see Graham's *Samuel Savage Sr. (c1655-1707), Stonemason, and His Descendants of Philadelphia, Berks and Chester Counties, Pennsylvania, Through Four Generations*, Ellicott City, MD, January 2004.

70  This should not be confused with Coventry House, which is still standing and per Cremers was built c.1733.

71  *The Potts Memorial*, pp. 50-51.

72  Estelle Cremers, *Coventry The Skool Kill District*, p. 73.

73  Rutter eventually obtained Adredus Rudman's entire 500-acre tract located in the far eastern section of Amity Township, Philadelphia County. *(Indenture, Pennsylvania Archives, Records of the Land Office, 1720, Samuel Goldy to Thomas Rutter, RG 17, Carton #3, Misc. Deeds, 1694-1834.)* His initial bloomery forge was built on the back 100 acres of this property and was converted to a refinery forge. When Douglass Township was formed about 1740, Thomas Potts, who then owned most of the forge, was instrumental in removing this tract from Amity Township and including it in Douglass with his other land. In 1752, it became part of Berks County. This area and ironworks would eventually be named Pine Forge.

74  For more information on Thomas Potts, see Graham's *Good Business Practices and Astute Match Making, The Ascendancy of Thomas Potts (c1680-1752) of Berks County, Pennsylvania in the Early Charcoal Iron Industry of Pennsylvania*, Ellicott City, MD, December 1997.

75  Henry Chapman Mercer, *The Bible in Iron*, Bucks County Historic Society, McGinty Co., Doylestown, 1914, pp. 33-34. Mercer calls the furnace on Rock Run: "Christine, alias Redding," "Christine, predecessor to Redding" or simply, "Christine-Redding." He does not indicate why he used Christine. Mercer does state that Christine was reconstructed or replaced by a new furnace built in 1736, but he confuses this with Branson's Reading Furnace. The name Christine is used in Coventry Forge books as a supplier of pig iron, but it is possible that this is Abington Furnace on Christiana Creek, also called Christiana Furnace, which Nutt and Branson were investors in.

76  *Records of the Land Office, Record Group 17, Letters of Attorney, Book D, #2*, p. 383.

77  Wilber MacEltree, *Around the Boundaries of Chester County*, Privately Printed, West Chester, PA, 1934, p. 507. I did not find this deed at the Chester County Archives. Thomas Potts died in 1785, three years before this deed. It was perhaps filed when his property was being distributed.

78  Estelle Cremers, *The Skool Kill District, A Brief History of the Three Coventry Townships 1700-1850*, Masthof Press, Morgantown, PA, 2003, p. 72.

79  Estelle Cremers, *Reading Furnace 1736*, p. 142. Cremers notes the original was in Berks County Court Pleadings and Miscellaneous Old Papers, 1802-1817. Lessee of John Penn and Richard Penn, Esq's, V. Mathew Brooke. Penn Claims Case, "Rachael Jones Affidavit."

80  *Records of the Land Office, Record Group 17, Letters of Attorney, Book D, #2*, pp. 382-383.

81   Several of the Lincoln family biographies indicate that Mordecai Lincoln married Robeson's sister, Mary as his second wife. However, a more recent source indicates Lincoln married Mary Millard, the daughter of Thomas Millard. James C. Landis, *Will the Real Mary Lincoln Please Stand Up?*, 1996, Private Printing.

82   MacEltree, p. 503.

83   *Pennsylvania Archives, Rock Run Furnace Account Book, 1743.*

84   *Library of Congress, American Memory, Pennsylvania Maps, 1700-1799.*

85   The term ironworks or just "works" was used to describe an industry that had at the same site more than a forge, generally a furnace, slitting or rolling mill. This industry was also called the Coventry Iron Works in early documents. It should be noted that a later works near Phoenixville was called the French Creek Works. Nutt always used the term "Iron-Works."

86   Thomas Chalkley, *A Collection of the Works of that Ancient, Faithful Servant of Jesus Christ, Thomas Chalkley*, 5th Edition, James Philips Printer, London, M,DCC,XCI, p. 185.

87   John Churchman, *An Account of the Gospel Labours, and Christian Experiences of a Faithful Minister of Christ, John Churchman, Late of Nottingham in Pennsylvania, Deceased*, James Philips printer, Philadelphia and London, 1731, p. 45.

88   Nutt's 1738 estate accounting of the company property he owned with William Branson does not list stove plates as an item. However, it does list "26 Forgg Plates." On his personal inventory, 18 stove plates are listed worth £8-6-0. Likewise, John Potts was making stoves and back plates at Rock Run Furnace in 1743, and none are known to exist. See Graham's 2012, *Colonial Pennsylvania Cast Iron Fire Backs, Stove Plates, and Warming Stoves 1726-1760*, County of Montgomery, Printer.

89   Henry Chapman Mercer, *The Bible in Iron*, p. 34.

90   Emanuel Swedenborg, *Regnum Subterraneum Sive Minerale De Ferro, Dresden and Lipsec*, Vol. II, 1734, p. 162, "Aliud majus ad fluvium Schulkill extruetum Dni Samuel Nuts, cum fornace & focis ferrariis." The translation was provided by Google. Published in 1736, it is unknown where and in what year Swedenborg obtained his information on Rutter, Nutt and Ball. He definitely has Nutt with a furnace as a singular and forge as a plural.

91   Carnegie Institution of Washington, *Proceedings and Debates of the British Parliaments Respecting North America: 1728-1739*, 1939, Vol. 338, p. 317.

92   *Newcastle County Deeds, H-1*, pp. 222-226. See J. Thomas Scharf, *History of Delaware, 1609-1888*, L. J. Richards, Philadelphia, 1888, Vol. 2, p. 951 for more information about Abington.

93 Charles H. Green, "Samuel Nutt," *The Sabbath Recorder*, Vol. 78, No. 19, May 10, 1915, pp. 582-584, and Albert N. Rogers, *Seventh Day Baptists in Europe and America*, Vol. II, American Tract Society, Plainfield, NJ, 1910, pp. 1111-1112.

94 *Pennsylvania Archives, Vol. 1*, pp. 215-216.

95 *Lawmaking & Legislators of Pennsylvania*, p. 786.

96 William W. Thompson, *Chester County and Its People*, the Union History Company, Chicago and New York, 1898, p. 476.

97 *American Weekly Mercury*, February 7, 1729.

98 Road Returns, Chester County Archives, Court Session August 1725.

99 *The Geology of Chester County*, J. Peter Leslie, Editor, Board of Commissioners, Harrisburg, PA, 1883, p. 29. Vincent River was the name given to French Creek on Holmes' 1685 map of Pennsylvania. It is used in early deeds or sometimes both are used: "Vincent River or French Creek."

100 Estelle Cremers, *30,000 Acres Vincent and Pikeland Townships 1686-1856*, Privately Printed, 1989.

101 Miriam Clegg, *The Nail Factory, Phoenixville Chester County, Pa.*, The Historical Society of the Phoenixville Area, 1981, p. 10.

102 Franklin Ellis and Samuel Evans, *History of Lancaster County*, Everts and Peck, Philadelphia, 1883, p. 311.

103 H. Frank Eshleman, "History of Lancaster County's Highway System," Papers Read Before the Lancaster County Historical Society, Vol. XXVI., No 1, 1922, p. 50. This road went by the old Jenkins Forge which may have prompted Branson to buy it. He sent Reading iron there.

104 *Minutes of the Provincial Council of Pennsylvania, Vol. IV*, Theo. Penn, printer, Harrisburg, 1851, pp. 152 and 266-273.

105 *Coventry Forge Ledger B, 1727-1730*, the earliest available forge book, shows that nearby farmer Michael Haldeman, who first appears on Coventry tax records in 1729, was supplying the company with farm provisions such as butter, meat, onions and eggs. These were traded for rum, molasses, and a bell. See *Pennsylvania German Roots across the Ocean*, Marion Egge, editor, Genealogical Society of Pennsylvania, 2000.

106 John Bezis-Selfa, "Slavery and the Disciplining of Free Labor in the Colonial Mid-Atlantic Iron Industry," Empire, Society and Labor, *Pennsylvania History: A Journal of Mid-Atlantic Studies*, Vol. 64, 1997, p. 273.

107  Samuel Gustaf Hermelin, *Report About the Mines in the United States of America, 1783;* translated from the Swedish with introduction and notes by Amandus Johnson, Published by John Morton Memorial Museum, Philadelphia, 1931, pp. 54-55. Gottlieb Mittleberger in his Journal for 1750, indicates the term of servitude for Germans was from two to six years and very young people, from 10 to 15 years, served until they were 21. See Mittleberger, *Journey to Pennsylvania in the Year 1750*, Translated by E. J. Eben, Philadelphia, 1898, p. 26-27.

108  *Pennsylvania Archives, Series 1, Vol. 3*, pp. 2678-2680.

109  *Votes and Proceedings of the House of Representatives, of the Province of Pennsylvania, Beginning the Fourteenth Day of October 1726, Vol. 3*, Printed and Sold by Ben. Franklin and D. Hall, MDCCLIV, pp. 1 and 3.

110  *Lawmaking & Legislators of Pennsylvania*, p. 786.

111  Gottlieb Mittleberger, p. 29.

112  J. Smith Futhey and Gilbert Cope, *History of Chester County, Pennsylvania*, Louis H. Everts publisher, Philadelphia, 1881, p. 344.

113  *Provincial Papers, Warranties of Land in the Several Counties of the State of Pennsylvania, Hard to Track Land Purchases, 1730-1898*, Edited by William Henry Engle, Vol. 1, Wm Stanley Ray, State Printer of Pennsylvania, 1898.

114  Futhey and Cope, p. 346.

115  Bucks County Historical Society, MSC 149, Folder 1, Item 4, Receipts for Payment of Surveys. Both John Potts, Sr. and John Potts, Jr. took efforts to ensure the land they purchased with Warwick Furnace had clear titles. Samuel Nutt was not as "conscientious" in obtaining title to his various tracks.

116  *Minutes of the Board of Property*, William Henry Egle, Editor, *Minute Book K*, Clarence M. Burch, State Printer, Harrisburg, 1894, p. 26.

117  Ibid., p. 55.

118  Ibid., p. 75.

119  Arthur Cecil Bining, Pennsylvania Iron Manufacture in the Eighteenth Century, Pennsylvania History and Museum Commission, Harrisburg, Pennsylvania, 1938, p. 40. In his 1933 *British Regulation of the Colonial Iron Industry*, Bining states this furnace was built in 1730 and uses as a reference: "Potts MSS, B. II, Coventry, 1728, pp. 214ff. passim, III, 1730 (1731-1732) pp. 132 ff. passim.," Batchelder indicates the furnace was built in 1734.

120  Hermelin, *Report About the Mines in the United States of America, 1783;* p. 1.

121  Futhey and Cope, p. 347.

122  *Pennsylvania Archives*, Samuel Hazzard, Joseph Sevens & Co., Philadelphia, Vol. 2, 1853, p. 57.

123  Morrison, Alfred J., Editor, *Travels in the Confederation, 1783-1784, from the German of Johann David Schoepf*, J. W. Campbell, Philadelphia, Pennsylvania, 1911, p. 6.

124  For a good write-up on Coventryville and its growth see the 1977 Coventryville Historic District write-up on file at the National Register of Historic Places by Mary Busenkill, Estelle Cremers, Eleanor Morris and others.

125  Batchelder, *The Memorial of Thomas Potts Junior*, p. 50. Batchelder seems to be originator of the Samuel Nutt, Jr. story. It has been routinely repeated by all secondary sources since the *Memorial's* publication.

126  *Pennsylvania Archives, Second Series, Vol. 8*, p. 225.

127  *Potts Memorial*, p. 93.

128  *Enterys of the Orphans Court of Chester County, Pennsylvania, 1716-1730, 1732-1734*, Transcribed by Miss Dorothy B. Lapp, Published by Richard T. and Mildred C. Williams, Danboro, Pennsylvania, 1973, pp. 103-105; and Gilbert Cope, *Genealogy of the Dunwoody and Hood Families*, Tribune Printing Company, 1899, pp. 61-62.

129  *Concord Monthly Meeting Records, 7mo 3, 1733, 8mo 8, 1733, and 12mo 4, 1733*, Swarthmore Friends Library.

130  *Pennsylvania Archives, Warrantees of Land, County of Chester 1733-1858, Third Series, Vol. 24*, p. 96.

131  *Chester County Deed, Book S*, p. 470.

132  *Chester County Deed, Book S*, p. 483.

133  *Judson, L. Carroll, A Biography of the Signers of the Declaration of Independence. Philadelphia, Pennsylvania, J. Dobson and Thomas, Coperthwait & Co. (1839). pp. 174-76. Carroll does not indicate where he found the Taylor indenture to Samuel Savage, but his biography routinely gets copied in most early works.*

134  James Duffin, *Guide to the Mortgages of the General Loan Office of the Province of Pennsylvania, 1724-1756*, Genealogical Society of Pennsylvania, Monograph Series no. 1, Genealogical Society of Pennsylvania, 1995, p. 21.

135  *Potts Memorial*, p. 61. Unfortunately, Batchelder only synopsizes the document and does not indicate what it was from and we don't get to see the entire document.

136 Although the spelling "Redding" was used in the John Potts document, Reading and a number of other spellings are used, often in the same document for both furnaces.

137 See MacEltree, pp. 506-507. I cannot find the original source that MacEltree used to come up with the property division as outlined in this illustration. It infers that in 1766, the French Creek Iron-Works company land was divided by Partition Proceedings between Thomas Potts, his father John Potts and the Heirs of William Branson, noted as Lynford Lardner, Et. Al. MacEltree indicates that Thomas Potts ended up with the forge property, John Potts with the old furnace property and the remaining land went to the Branson heirs.

138 Samuel Nutt's original inventory is located at the Chester County Archives but has some water damage and is hard to read. Susannah Brody provides the complete transcript of the inventory in her biography of Nutt in *Prosperous Beginnings, Chester County Biographies.*

139 William M. Reynolds, Editor, *History of New Sweden*, Israel Acrelius, Historical Society of Pennsylvania, 1874, p. 165.

140 Chester County Estate Papers. The inventory is noted as: "An Inventory of the Estate of the Widow Nutt Relict of Samuel Nutt Senr Late of Coventry Deceasd And Samuel Nutt Junior Late of Coventry Deceased in Company with Wm Branson Taken and Appraised This 12 Day of February 1739/40."

141 Robert Grace's involvement at Coventry and Warwick was famously mentioned in Benjamin Franklin's autobiography: "In Order of Time I should have mentioned before, that having in 1742 invented an open Stove, for the better warming of Rooms and at the same time saving Fuel, as the fresh Air admitted was warmed in Entering, I made a Present of the Model to Mr. Robert Grace, one of my early Friends, who having an Iron Furnace, found the Casting of the Plates for these Stoves a profitable Thing." See Benjamin Franklin, *Memoirs of the Life and Writings of Benjamin Franklin*, Henry Colburn, London, 1818, p. 94.

142 Thomas Savage had obtained this land in 1734. James Steel, Regr. Genl., noted on 7Mo. 3, 1734: "Recd. of Thomas Savage Twenty Pounds in part for a Tract of Two Hundred Acres of Land Surveyed to Nicholas Rogers...the said Tract of Land Lyes on a branch of the French Creek."

143 "Pig Iron Marketed in 1738-'39," *The Perkiomen Region Past and Present*, Adams Apple Press, Bedminister, PA, 1994, Volumes I, II, and III, September 1894-April 1901, p. 46.

144 Bucks County Historical Society, MSC 149, Folder 1, Item 7, Copy of receipts for pig iron sent by Anna Nutt from the Warwick Furnace for the account of Thomas Penn, November 1739.

145 Indenture, 5 May 1740 and 6 May 1740, Pottstown Historical Society.

146  A variety of dates have been given for the construction date of Coventry House. It is generally agreed that it is the house Rebecca (Savage) Nutt and Robert Grace moved into after their 1740 marriage. The Rock Run Ledger has an entry for August 1743 paying Henry Hockley for six bushels of lime to plaster the "new house." This is possibly Coventry House.

147  Futhey and Cope, pp. 344-345.

148  Ibid., p. 245. It is interesting to note the furnace at Rock Run was probably closed by this time or already closed. John Potts was running it the following year.

149  Bucks County Historical Society. Lease and Articles of Agreement Warwick Furnace, MSC 149, Folder 1.

# INDEX